Dick Sutphen's
Master of Life Manual

Valley of the Sun Publishing, Box 38, Malibu, CA 90265

The dialogues in
this book are from the
Bushido® and **Master of Life®** **Seminars.**
For Information,
Write:
Sutphen Seminars
Box 38
Malibu, CA 90265

First Printing: January, 1980
Fifth Printing: January, 1987
145,000 copies in print

Additional copies of Dick **Sutphen's Master of Life Manual** are available by mail for $3.95 each. Send check or money order, plus $1.50 per order postage and handling, to: Valley of the Sun Publishing Co., Box 38, Malibu, California 90265. A catalog of over 350 tapes and books is also available.

ISBN: 911842-18-7
Library of Congress Catalog Card Number: 86-51640

*To those who
seek awareness
within*

This book is written for a very special New Age race of people willing to sacrifice what they are for what they might become. The awareness is an introduction to the concepts that serve as the premise of the Sutphen Seminar Trainings, and encourages you to explore your viewpoints in relation to reality. Dick incorporates the Eastern concepts of karma, reincarnation, Zen, Tao and Wu-Wei into workable Western principles of self-responsibility, freedom and unconditional love. Now in its fifth printing, **The Master of Life Manual** has become an international underground bestseller.

CONTENTS

YOUR MIND

A man kept a goose in a bottle, feeding it until it grew too large to get through the bottleneck. How can he get the goose out of the bottle without killing it or destroying the bottle?

This Zen koan offers a choice between two alternatives, both of which are equally impossible. The purpose of the koan is to reflect the dilemma of life: The problem of passing beyond the two alternatives of assertion and denial, both of which obscure the truth. The real problem is not to get the goose out of the bottle, but rather to get ourselves out of it. The goose represents man and the bottle, his circumstances. Our bottleneck is our conditioned way of seeing things. We see situations and problems as alien objects standing in our way rather than as an extension of our own consciousness. We are conditioned to believe that our mind is inside us and that our perceptions of the world are outside. In reality, our mind is outside and all that we perceive is within our mind. Or, to put it another way, "The goose is out!"

*The world is passing
through a stage
of evolution*

Into a new age:

From hatred to love.

1.
HOW YOU WORK

Everyone reading this book is already a **Master of Life**—a happy, self-confident, fearless, self-actualized individual. You are above all the problems in your life, but you don't realize it because—like almost everyone else on this planet—you've accepted layer upon layer of fear-based programming:

- Anxiety
- Anger
- Jealousy
- Hate
- Repression
- Envy
- Greed
- Possessiveness
- Arrogance

- Guilt
- Insecurity
- Inhibitions
- Egotism
- Vanity
- Malice
- Resentment
- Blame
- ... and on ... and on ... and on!

My goal in this overly simplified little volume is to prove to you that you are already a self-actualized **Master of Life,** and to point to some logical awareness that, if accepted, can assist you to remove the fears that block you from expressing unconditional love and keep you from becoming all you are capable of being.

So, to begin at the beginning, you need to be aware that every thought you've ever had, every word you've ever spoken, and every action you've ever experienced is recorded in the memory banks of your subconscious mind. This also includes all the memories of previous lifetimes.

According to brain researchers, the subconscious mind has 200,000 times the capacity of the largest computer ever built, so recording the history of your lives really isn't too great a task. In addition, it is now known that the human mind works like a computer, so all your past experiences represent your software programming. It is this programming that has made you what you are today. Your talents and abilities, problems and afflictions are the result of this subconscious programming. Your subconscious has directed you and it will continue to direct you. Sadly, it is often in opposition to your conscious desires. For example:

You'd like to be able to go boating with your friends, but for some reason, you experience a great deal of anxiety whenever you get into a boat. Consciously, you realize there is minimal danger in boating, yet the anxiety persists.

Why? Because the subconscious has no reasoning power. It simply operates . . . like a computer. It functions as the result of programming. Maybe you experienced a fearful, though forgotten, trauma involving water as a child, or maybe you drowned in a past life. The result was negative programming, and although the past experience may not relate today, you still experience the anxiety.

The subconscious creates only according to its programming. It will assist to bring into actuality the reality for which it is programmed. This may have nothing to do with what you consciously desire, relating only to the past programming (thoughts and experiences) it has received.

If the subconscious were to receive no new programming, it would continue to operate on past input. This, of course, cannot happen, for you are constantly feeding new programming or data into your subconscious mind— **your computer.** Every thought programs the computer. Thus, if your thoughts are more negative than positive, your computer is being programmed negatively. **You create your own reality, or karma, with your thoughts.**

Many people have no idea how frequently they think in a negative manner. If you climb out of bed cursing the alarm clock, grumble your way through breakfast, then dwell on how much you dislike the rain and the traffic during your commute to work, and brood unhappily about your job, and on and on throughout the day, you are literally creating a worse reality for yourself. Because you are thinking more negative thoughts than positive ones, there is simply no way you can be creating anything but a negative reality. With all that negative programming of your computer, how could it do anything but create the programmed result: more negativity?

You do not **have** a mind, you **are** mind. You are using your current body, but your body isn't you. You have a soul or a spirit or whatever you want to call it. Whatever it is, it must be mind, for any study of regressive hypnosis will show that the mind carries all the memories of the past. Every individual carries memories of previous lifetimes, and the events in these past lives often seem to be affecting the present. This in itself does not prove reincarnation, but does show that a lineage of cause and effect (karma) is evident.

If you are mind and that mind operates like a computer, that makes you a computer ... a machine. Naturally, there is more to you than the mechanical aspect, but few people are presently working with the larger aspects of their totality.

To become a Master of Life means to transform the way you experience your life. In so doing, you learn to let fear and negativity flow through you without affecting you, and to be direct and natural, in balance and harmony.

Everyone has the potential to create their own reality, so if you are not happy with the way it is, what mind has created, mind can change. To better understand these concepts, the following information shows how effectively the subconscious mind programs us. The subconscious mind doesn't reason but it does appear to generate circumstances to create a reality that reflects the programming it receives. Although this is normally accomplished by thoughts and through our life experiences, brain researchers have found that the subconscious is incapable of telling the difference between reality and fantasy ... between the real experience and the imagined experience.

REALITY/FANTASY TESTS

One of the initial tests that proved this was the recording of the actual brain wave patterns under specific conditions. Test subjects would be placed in a room and wired up to an EEG machine. Someone would now run into the room and fire a gun. Someone else would do a dance, a dog would bark, a color would be projected and many other test situations were created. As the test subject was exposed to each situation, it caused his brain waves to form patterns on the recording instruments. Each situation was marked on the recording paper so the researchers would know what had transpired to create each pattern. "Dog barked here," as an example.

The next stage of the test was to have the subject sit and concentrate upon the situations described by the researchers. As an example, "I now want you to imagine yourself watching a woman doing a dance. See it in your mind, fantasize it, conceive it with as much imagination as possible. . . . All right, I now want you to imagine a dog barking."

While the subject was concentrating upon these imagined situations, his brain waves were once again being recorded. The results of the tests showed the exact same patterns of up and down brain waves were created when

12

the woman came into the room and did a dance as when the subject imagined her doing a dance. The same was true with all other situations with all of the test subjects.

The brain waves were identical, so the computer part of the brain was obviously incapable of telling the real from the imagined.

USING THE KNOWLEDGE

Another supportive series of tests were conducted by the University of Chicago. These and many similar tests show how our subconscious computer actually creates the reality for which it is programmed. Three test groups of subjects took part in a mental programming experiment based upon shooting a basketball. All the participating students were tested as to their individual basket-shooting ability and the results were recorded.

Group One was told, "Don't play any basketball for a month. In fact, just forget about basketball for the entire month."

Group Two was told, "You are each to practice shooting baskets for one full hour a day, every day, for the month."

Group Three was told, "You are to spend one hour a day imagining you are successfully shooting baskets. Do this every day for the month. Imagine or fantasize yourself at being successful shooting baskets. See every detail of your accomplishments in your mind."

One month later, the three groups were again tested as to their basket-shooting ability. The Group One participants, who hadn't played basketball for a month, tested exactly the same as they did the first time. Group Two, who had been practicing a full hour every day for a month, demonstrated a 24-percent improvement in their basket-shooting ability. Group Three, who had only imagined that they were successfully shooting baskets for an hour each day, tested 23 percent improved in their actual basket-shooting ability—only one percentage point less than the group that had actually been practicing.

Obviously, the group that only imagined shooting baskets successfully programmed their subconscious computer to perform almost as effectively as those who had actually practiced. **The computer assisted in creating the reality it was programmed to set into motion.** The subconscious can be fooled. It can be tricked. It can be programmed—you simply have to know how to become the programmer. This is one of the reasons hypnosis works so effectively as a reprogramming technique.

All right, let's carry the concept of your being a machine a little farther. Your entire past has programmed the you that is reading this. You are the programmer of your machine.

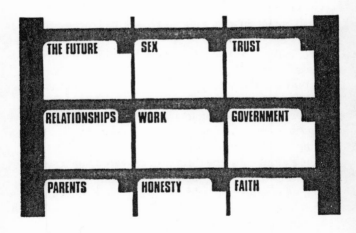

THE FUTURE   SEX   TRUST

RELATIONSHIPS   WORK   GOVERNMENT

PARENTS   HONESTY   FAITH

1. There are thousands of categories in your computer. Each is already programmed by your past thoughts and experiences.

THE FUTURE

My Immediate Future
The Future Of My Marriage
My Monetary Future
My Future Health
My Future Career
The Country's Future

SEX

General Attitude
Intercourse With Mate
Intercourse With Others
Masturbation
Fantasies
Pornography

2. Each category is broken into many subcategories which are also programmed by your past thoughts and experiences. You have feelings about all of these things. You have a viewpoint in respect to every category and subcategory in your computer. As you look at these illustrations, you internally respond to each example. There are thousands and thousands of categories in your computer.

3. You have a conscious **viewpoint** regarding every category. The way that you have arrived at this **viewpoint** is the result of your past thoughts and experiences.

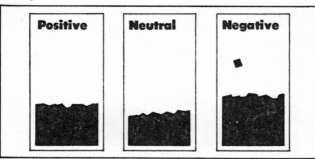

15

4. Since you program your computer with your thoughts and experiences, let's look more closely at that for a moment. Symbolically, each category and subcategory has programming slots for positive, neutral and negative input. Every bit of input (thought) adds more programming to that slot. In the illustration, a negative thought is dropping into the negative programming slot. When enough input is received in that particular slot, the computer will create the negative reality for which it was programmed. Let's say the thought above is a complaint about your primary relationship. If the computer receives far more negative than positive input in this category, eventually the negative slot will fill up and the computer will assist in creating a separation or divorce.

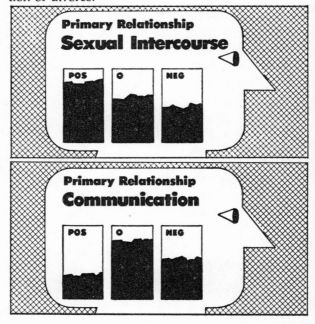

5. Every computer category is going to have many sub-categories. In the above illustration, we have two subcategories of the Primary Relationship Category. In actuality, there would be many more, such as Shared Interests, Common Goals, Attitude Toward Children, etc.

6. In this illustration, the subcategories have been totaled and we can oberve the overall programming of the Primary Relationship category at this time. In this case, there is a little more negative than positive input, which says that the relationship is going downhill. If it isn't stabilized and moved into the positive programming realms, the eventual result could be separation or divorce. Positive begets positive and negative begets negative.

7. You quite literally create your experiences by the way you have programmed your computer in the past. This is karma. Karma doesn't need to be mystical—cause and effect is simple logic, being nothing but the past programming of your subconscious computer. Since you create your experiences with your thoughts, it boils down to one very loud, clear, simple fact: **You—and you alone—are responsible for everything that happens to you.**

8. You created the reality you are now living. How do you like it? Are you happy with the job you did on yourself, or do you wish you'd planned it a little better in some areas? The areas of your life that you have programmed well are those areas that work well. You are fulfilled, centered and happy in these areas and things work the way they are supposed to work. You're happy with the results. The areas of your life that are not working well are the areas you have programmed poorly in the past.

9. All right, let's get back to your **viewpoint.** The past programming in any category has resulted in a conscious viewpoint—your feelings, opinions, anxieties, fears and attitudes toward a particular subject. **This viewpoint is totally based upon your past experiences.** That is the only way you could have a viewpoint. What you need to realize is that your viewpoint is distorted, because there is no way for you to have all the facts on anything. Your past experiences have prejudiced your viewpoint. Obviously, everyone has a different viewpoint. Although the subject may be the same, there is no way for any two people to have experienced exactly the same computer input, so everyone's viewpoint is different. And everyone's viewpoint is distorted with respect to the facts.

10. To carry this a little farther, realize that not only does your conscious mind have a viewpoint on every category in your life, **but your subconscious mind also has a viewpoint on every category in your life.** Your subconscious viewpoint is also distorted, and often your conscious and subconscious viewpoints are out of alignment with each other. There is a contradiction between the two and the result is a problem area in your life.

   Example 1: As a child, you were told that "sex is bad," resulting in negative sexual programming of the sub-

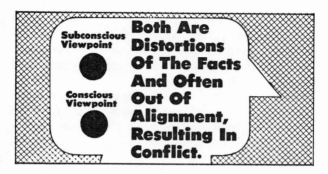

Subconscious Viewpoint

Conscious Viewpoint

Both Are Distortions Of The Facts And Often Out Of Alignment, Resulting In Conflict.

conscious mind. As an adult, you consciously desire a good sexual relationship but you experience problems.

Example 2: You once failed in a long-forgotten project, which resulted in subconscious fear of failure programming. As an adult, you desire success but your career is mediocre.

All right, let's look at this programming again. Your conscious viewpoint was programmed by your past thoughts and experiences that took place between the time you were born and the present moment. You may remember this programming consciously ... or you may not.

Your subconscious viewpoint is a little different. It too is the result of all your thoughts and experiences in the life you are now living, but it also remembers every detail of every experience of your past lives.

11. Back to your conscious and subconscious viewpoints. You generally understand how they are programmed. We have provided two examples of misalignment of the conscious and subconscious in the context of the present life. Now, let's look at the same situation ... but with misaligned viewpoints based on experiences from a past life.

Example 1: A woman with sleep problems con-

19

sciously wants to experience a good night's sleep, but it doesn't happen. During regression, she relives a life in ancient Greece in which a rapist attacked her while she was sleeping, resulting in subconscious programming that is affecting her present life.

Example 2: A possessive man is destroying his marriage, but seems unable to control his emotions in this area. In regression, he relives a turn-of-the-century life as a woman who lost her husband to a younger, more beautiful woman.

MAGNITUDE 1 EXPERIENCE

**SHOCK
PHYSICAL PAIN
EXTENSIVE
MENTAL PAIN
Or any combination**

12. Past experiences create layers of fear. The subconscious computer is programmed with fear experiences and the **original self-actualized person is smothered by the layers of garbage.** The real you becomes lost under all the programming.

In many cases, such as the examples represented, there is one primary experience that has created the problem within you. This is what I call a **Magnitude 1 Experience.**

There are many levels or magnitudes of experience, but a Mag 1 experience is extremely traumatic and includes shock, physical pain, extensive mental pain or any combination of these elements. Mag 1 experiences result in extensive programming of your computer and the result is often a hang-up, a phobia, or some form of problem effect that relates back to the original situation. These kinds of experiences can destroy your life. They can so distort your reality as to make the unreal real and the real unreal. It can twist your perceptions to such a degree that you literally cannot relate to the facts ... to the way things actually are in particular categories of your computer.

*Man is like an onion,
evolving by stripping away
the layers of anger,
selfishness, jealousy,
hate, repression, envy,
greed, possessiveness,
anxiety, guilt, insecurity,
inhibitions, egotism, vanity,
malice, resentment, blame,
and arrogance...
until there is nothing left
but the True Self.*

REINCARNATION

Reincarnation is the subject for an entire book, and I've written several on the subject*, so I will not attempt to explain the concept again in a few pages. I do want to point out that I don't feel reincarnation is necessarily a matter of living a physical lifetime and then dying and returning to another lifetime as a sequential series of physical incarnations. It may very well be that we are the result of a spiritual, genetic lineage of lifetimes. If this is the situation, it really doesn't change anything, for these previous lives appear to be affecting the present. In **Past Lives, Future Loves** (Pocket Books), I describe seven different possibilities as to how reincarnation might work.

My experience in regressing thousands of people is that everyone, regardless of their belief systems, carries complete memories of other lifetimes, and that these past-life incidents are affecting the present.

Examples of common negative karmic carryovers:

1. Tension headaches or migraine problems often relate to a past life in which the victim was clubbed, guillotined, stoned, hanged or hurt in some way that was fatal to the neck or head.

2. Depressions or emotional problems with physical carryovers often trace back to tragedies with strong guilt associations.

3. Weight problems often result from a lifetime of starvation, or from a lifetime in which the victim's good looks caused him or her to be hurt or killed.

You Were Born Again To Be Together, Past Lives, Future Loves, and *Unseen Influences* are published by Simon Schuster Pocket Books. *We, Immortals,* by Alan Weisman, is the story of the early Sutphen Seminars and is also published by Pocket Books. *Past-Life Therapy In Action,* with co-author Lauren Leigh Taylor and *Enlightenment Transcripts* are published by Valley of the Sun Publishing Company.

4. Troubled marital relationships often relate to the same couple being together in a previous lifetime in which they hurt each other.

5. Abdominal pains frequently relate to past-life incidents of being shot or stabbed in the stomach, or to a painful operation in times when surgery was an imperfect procedure.

Examples of common positive karmic carryovers:

1. Natural talent in a particular area, such as art, music, sports, or salesmanship usually relates to a pattern of development through several lifetimes.

2. A happy, fulfilled, long-term man/woman relationship that happened naturally, without transformation of the couple's viewpoint, often relates to harmonious prior relationships.

3. A position of influence with masses of people is usually earned by experience in previous times.

In seminar trainings, I ask, "If you do not believe in reincarnation, don't let it block experiencing. Simply flow with the regressions and judge by what you experience. You will perceive past-life situations, and judge if you feel they relate to you by the seemingly valid expanded awareness or the anxiety-releasing results."

KARMA

Cause and effect: "As you sow, so shall you reap." If you throw a rock in the lake, you are the cause and the splash is the effect ... and the splash now becomes the cause of the ripples which are an effect. Before you, there was the volcanic eruption that created the rock, and there was the river that carried it downstream ... and so it goes, back into infinity.

The chain of cause and effect traces everything that has ever happened in the universe back to some original cause. The effects you are reaping now, both positive and negative, are the results of causes from this lifetime or from previous lifetimes. The seeds (causes) you are sowing now will bring forth the effects yet to come in this lifetime or future lifetimes. Your entire life, your state of mind, health, relationships with others, money you have or haven't made ... all are effects. Somewhere in your background, these effects were set into motion by causes that were set into motion by your mind.

Karma works both ways—it rewards as well as punishes. I don't like the word punish, for a negative event or situation in your life is really only an opportunity. The event is not important; what is important is how you react to the event, what you think about what has happened. If you react in a positive way, you are erasing your karma. You have learned your past lesson; you have learned wisdom and wisdom erases karma. If you respond to the event in a negative way, with bitterness, remorse, revenge, etc., you have not learned your lesson, and sometime in your future, you will have to once again come up against the "opportunity." When I say future, I mean this lifetime or lifetimes to come.

Until we have learned from the past, we are destined to repeat it. Learning is the process of remembering the past.

Every mistake, every failure, is really a success. We achieve true success only by learning from our failures. If you fell off a bike twenty times before you succeeded in riding it, you needed twenty failures to learn to succeed. The sooner you fall twenty times, the sooner you succeed.

TOTAL JUSTICE

If there is meaning to life beyond that which we can substantiate with science, then there must be a reason or plan. Logically, it follows that justice exists as part of such a plan. But look around you—instead of justice, you see greed, dishonesty and manipulation rewarded, and there is simply no explanation for the cruel injustice that is evidenced everywhere.

Organized religion would have us believe that if we're good, we'll go to heaven. And if we're bad, we go below. Let's examine this concept with an example of inequality: Once upon a time, there was a little girl who was born into a well-to-do and happy family. She grew up to marry a good man and lived a happy, healthy life. She had several children and died a peaceful death at an old age. Now, let's look at another child, a girl who is born into poverty. She is crippled, never experiences happiness and dies a lingering, painful death at an early age. Religion says that she will find her reward in heaven. Does that mean that the other girl, who had a happy and full life, is to be punished or find lesser rewards in heaven? Or if both find the same heaven, how can the life of misery be justified?

Karma, being totally just, fully explains the supposed inequality. The crippled girl needed to learn some lessons from the sad life, or she needed to balance something she had done in a previous incarnation.

Perhaps she lived a lifetime as a woman in the 1890's in London, where she gave birth to a child she didn't want. She maintained the child for three months, until times became hard for her. At that time, she simply abandoned her baby without ensuring his proper care. As a result, the baby contracted a lung disease which eventually resulted in death at an early age. From a karmic perspective, this woman needed to learn what it felt like to be an unwanted child, and to experience some of the pain she had so thoughtlessly inflicted on another. Thus she incarnated as the crippled girl previously described. Yet no one needs to literally experience "an eye for an eye" if they can learn

25

through understanding and love.

What about heaven and hell? This indicates there is a dividing line. If you are just good enough, you'll make it to heaven; a few degrees less good and you go to hell. The metaphysical belief is that heaven and hell are of your own making here on earth or on the other side. The devil is a fear-based morality concept used to control masses of people. If you need fear to keep you in line, you can accept it—and, in fact, create a very real devil in your life. Yet it exists only because you give it power.

LEARNING

We are conditioned to learn through pain. We touch a hot stove and burn our fingers. We touch it again and burn our fingers again. After several encounters with the stove, we come to know intuitively—due to our painful past experiences—that hot stoves are not to be touched.

What if you first met your current mate in ancient China and the relationship was violent and painful. And then you reincarnated together in early Rome and again experienced extremely negative interaction. In thirteenth-century England, you went another round together. And so it has gone, lifetime after lifetime, until now. Here you are, back together again, and it's a lot better than it was in ancient China. You still fight and cause each other unnecessary anxiety, but you are still learning. Intuitively, you remember the past pain and attempt to avoid inflicting it on each other again. In a few more lifetimes, you might evolve beyond the negativity and share a happy, fulfilling relationship.

It's sad we believe we have to learn this way when it is possible to learn through understanding, love and wisdom. Wisdom erases karma. The acceptance and incorporation of the Master of Life philosophy into your life assists you to begin to rise above fear and negativity, and open to expressing unconditional love.

"*How* shall I escape from the wheel
of Birth and Death?"
The master replied,
"Who put you under restraint?"

The mind is
its own place,
and of itself
can make a
heaven of hell,
a hell of heaven.

2.
MASTER OF LIFE BASICS

RESISTANCE

Man's isolation and problems result from his means of resisting life. There is a universal law of resistance that says: **"What you resist, you draw to yourself. As long as you resist something, you are locked into it and you perpetuate its influence in your life."**

The ancient teachings of Wu-Wei tell the secret of mastering circumstances without asserting oneself against them. Martial arts are based upon these concepts. The principle is to yield to an oncoming force in such a way as to render it harmless, and at the same time change its direction by pushing it from behind instead of resisting it from the front. Relating this to everyday living, the Master of Life doesn't oppose things; he doesn't attempt to change things by asserting himself against them. Instead, he goes with the flow, yielding to its full force and either pushing it slightly out of direct line or moving it around in the opposite direction without ever encountering its direct opposition. This is the principle of controlling life by going along with it.

The first thing to understand about resistance is not to resist "what is." Some things are facts. Income taxes exist ... that's what is. Gravity exists ... that's what is. You can spend your time attempting to change what is, but there isn't much you're going to do about it. If you're married to a quiet, stubborn man, you can resist that fact and frustrate yourself, wanting him to be other than what he is, or you can accept what is and make your life easier. Resistance is fear.

FEAR

There is only one problem that exists between human beings: fear. Fear is responsible for all disturbances, large or small, international or interpersonal. Hatred, anger, possessiveness, tension, anxiety, greed, inhibition, stress, frustrations, hang-ups, phobias, insecurities . . . all are fear-based emotions.

Example 1: Sally and John are having a fight. She is upset because he isn't willing to escort her to the ten-year reunion. Fear: Sally is fearful of going alone, probably because she fears what other people will "think" about her going alone. Anger is always fear and obviously she wants John to be something other than what he is. She is angry because he is not willing to conform to her idea of what he should be—a husband who takes his wife to the reunion. When we expect people to be other than what they are, we are resisting life.

Example 2: One country declares war on another country. Fear: The warring nation fears not having enough of something—land, resources or control . . . or maybe it was the personal insecurity of the power-hungry leader.

Accepting that the only problem between people is fear, we can simplify even more. **There is only one fear: The fear of being unable to cope with a situation.** Do you believe you fear rejection? It isn't the rejection that you fear; it's not being able to cope with it. Do you fear rattlesnakes? It isn't the snake you fear, but coping with such an encounter.

Another thing to be aware of in regard to fear: You never fear what is; you only fear the **future** possibility. For example:

You're out in the desert and you're afraid of meeting a rattlesnake. You encounter a snake and then you're afraid it's going to bite you. It bites you and then you're afraid you're going to die. Each new aspect of fear relates to a future potential, not the situation of the moment.

Fear paralyzes us and keeps us from acting when we need to act. It can stop us from making a growth choice when it would be in our best interest. In accepting the fear and living with it, **you are imprisoned within it.**

Courage is a matter of being afraid and choosing to act anyway. The Master of Life would choose to fully experience his fear, while knowingly observing every internal reaction of his discomfort: **total experience.** By allowing the fear to be, it lets you be and you negate the law of resistance. You rise above the effects of the fear; it simply disappears.

When you choose not to act because of fear, you begin to avoid life, and life becomes nothing but what remains after all the avoidances. If you avoid enough of life and let it become very dull and boring, you can be sure that eventually your mind will do something to make life exciting. Maybe an illness—kidney stones will give you something to talk about. Or a tragic accident could stimulate you into an awareness of living. Remember, in resisting, you magnetize what you resist and draw it to you.

Life is a game—a series of things to do. If you don't have things to do—a purpose and reason for living—**you die.** We need to take risks to live for without risks there is no game, and without a game to play, there is no life.

The following quote by Helen Keller summarizes this concept: "Security is mostly a superstition. It does not exist in nature, nor do the children of men as a whole experience it. Avoiding danger is no safer in the long run than out right exposure. Life is either a daring adventure or nothing."

LOVE

If fear is the problem, love is the solution. Love is the ultimate power. And since love is power, fear is weakness. With this in mind, let's look at love in regard to our primary relationships.

Most of us are jealous, possessive and envious, yet we call this love. Can a possessive or envious individual really love, or is he protecting his own pleasure and thus operating out of fear? Most of the love I've seen is fear. That means **the fear of losing.** In addition, where there is fear, there is aggression. So most "love" relationships include a great deal of aggression.

Any love relationship based upon **"need"** is based upon **avoiding losing.** This obviously engages the law of resistance, so if you're resisting loss, you automatically begin to program that loss.

Being totally idealistic, what would **"unconditional love"** be like?

To begin with, it could not be diminished by anything the other person said or did. Your love would not be dependent upon being loved. You would give freely, without any expectation of return. In an environment of "real love," you would allow total freedom to your mate, expecting no more than the other could give. You would love for what the other was. You would not expect your mate to change, to be something he or she was not. You would find joy in the other's happiness. Only when there is love for oneself can there be love for others. To experience loving yourself, you need to know who you really are beneath your fears, and you need to accept yourself.

Then when you love someone, you can find joy in the positive aspects of your relationship and allow the negatives to simply flow past you without affecting you.

What a beautiful relationship this involved detachment would be. By accepting and granting freedom, not out of indifference but out of tenderness and caring, a couple can overcome karma and evolve beyond the level of problems. Since you would no longer be affected by the problems, you would no longer have the problems. Karma would be balanced, and your own wisdom would have erased the need for further learning.

If fear is the problem, love is the solution. Universal love. A goal of everyone now living upon the earth is to rise above the effects of fear and learn love. Most are unaware of this fact, but it is a reason why we are reborn, over and over. We all subconsciously seek love and its perfection. If we cannot remember what we have forgotten, we will be given another chance to learn, when we are together again.

POSSESSIVENESS

Man suffers because of his craving to possess and keep forever things which are essentially impermanent: his own person, loved ones and material things. All things are impermanent, and as soon as man tries to possess them, they slip away. As in trying to grasp water, the tighter you clutch, the faster it slips through your fingers.

Those who attempt to possess are themselves **possessed.** They are slaves to their own illusions about life. Possessiveness is a denial of the right of people and things to live and change. Thus, the possessor loses.

By accepting the Master of Life philosophy, you will lose the need to possess. The Master of Life joins "self" and "life" into so close a unity and rhythm that the distinction between the two is forgotten. He abandons the desire to possess for he knows that no one can possess and nothing can be possessed. He no longer grasps at things that flow by in the stream of life. Instead, he goes with the flow of the current, becoming one with it, aware that all things are simply waves in the water and to try to clutch them will only make them disappear.

CONSCIOUS DETACHMENT

A problem doesn't need to be eliminated to be solved. Perspective or your personal viewpoint is the solution to most problems. Because when you are no longer affected by a problem, you no longer have a problem, although nothing about the problem situation may outwardly have changed. For example:

You work with someone you dislike; every day he calls you names. He says, "You're a frog-faced son of a toad who eats bugs." Now you accept it and let it affect you. You get upset because you can't separate things in an enlightened way. First, you must realize that it isn't what someone says or does to you, short of physical violence, that affects you—it is only what **you think about what they say** that affects you. Why allow someone else's lack of balance to affect your balance? Why allow someone else's problem to create a problem in you? To do so is to hurt yourself. You can only hurt yourself by accepting what they said. Now project this thinking into all aspects of your life. The person closest to you is often warm and loving, and you enjoy these times, but this person can also be selfish and self-centered. So, during those times, you detach mentally and let the negativity flow past you without affecting you. It is that person's right to be grouchy, and it is your right not to be affected. Nothing about the situation has changed except the way you view it.

Another important item to remember is that what anyone says to you comes out of their past and past-life conditioning, from the memory banks of their computer. Thus it is their viewpoint and cannot directly relate to you. The way they relate to you, they would relate to anyone who represented to them what you represent. For example:

Mary's father was very cruel to her mother. She grew up fearing him and developed the attitude that "all husbands are S.O.B.'s," as she stated in a counseling session after her third divorce. Her computer's viewpoint is that "all husbands are S.O.B.'s" and any man in the position of being her husband is going to be perceived in this way. Naturally, each man took it personally, and fights and conflicts ensued. In reality, it wasn't personal—any man Mary married would be an "S.O.B."

Don't take anyone else's reactions to you personally. They see you through their own veils of opinions and conclusions. Be aware that you also see others the same way. No one is capable of accurate perceptions. Others' reactions to you are nothing but statements of their viewpoints, having nothing to do with the facts or the way things actually are.

COMPASSION

Compassion: A feeling of deep sympathy and sorrow for another's suffering or misfortune, accompanied by a desire to alleviate the pain or remove its cause (Random House Dictionary).

Ideally, when you find yourself experiencing compassion for another human being, you will assist by creating conditions within which they can choose to alleviate their own pain. You can experience the anguish of another's suffering, but you must live with the helpless knowledge that you can do nothing to save them from their pain. Everyone is totally responsible for everything that happens to them, thus their pain is their choice and they are the only ones who can choose not to experience it.

The degree of compassion you feel will depend upon how much you care for each person, and very likely, whether or not they accept responsibility for their condition. The question is, are they willing to do something to resolve the situation? If they are, you can assist by offering encouragement, creating a space for them to rise above the effects of their difficulty.

JUDGMENT/TRUTH/AWARENESS

We judge everything through our **viewpoint.** We call it right, wrong, moral or immoral, ethical or unethical. Maybe several of us, or even the majority of us, agree to call it the same thing. That doesn't make it truth. That is only what it is to us: **our truth.** Our agreeing that it is moral doesn't make it moral; it simply makes it what we **call** moral, it cannot change what it actually is.

There is no such thing as truth. "Truth" exists only as it relates to you. "Truth is not what we discover, but what we create," according to Antoine de St. Exupery.

Let's assume we are in a seminar training in a large hotel ballroom. I think the temperature is perfect—that's **my** truth. When I ask for a show of hands, one third of the group thinks it is too cold in the room; that's **their** truth. Half the group thinks it is too warm in the room; that's **their** truth. Each person has his own truth . . . and it has nothing to do with the **fact.** The fact is that it is 74 degrees in the room.

Life is filled with philosophical truths which we all commonly accept and rarely challenge. Yet these outdated truths, notions, views and moralities are restricting our lives. A good example is the idea that if you make a mistake or have a fault, you should feel guilty. Why should guilt be associated with making an honest mistake?

Let's look at the ultimate truth, the golden rule: "Do unto others as you would have them do unto you." How could anyone disagree with such a beautiful idea? Yet as any counselor will tell you, there are a lot of people out there who enjoy experiencing some pretty strange things. Sadomasochistic pleasures associated with the infliction of pain are only one extreme example. I certainly wouldn't want these people doing unto me as they would have done unto them. Remembering that we create in our lives exactly what we need to experience, look at how most of those around you experience their primary relationships. In how many do you see a self-inflicted source of anguish and anxiety? Do you want them to do unto you as they obviously want done unto them?

If you accept philosophical truths as valid, you accept restrictions ... **you accept traps.** A trap is an assumption, accepted without challenge, and it will keep you enslaved until you do challenge. In your life, you are probably accepting many truths that are holding you back.

Example 1: You work as a salesman for a company and you accept that you're a good salesman, yet not as good as the top man. That acceptance is a trap which will keep you from ever becoming the top salesman.

Example 2: You'd like to write a book, but feel that you don't have the perseverance it will take to complete the project. Your belief becomes your reality.

Something else to remember about truth: Just because a concept is repeated over and over and over again doesn't make it truth. There are numerous metaphysical organizations which claim to teach esoteric truths. They capitalize Truth and treat it as sacred. They may agree on the most general overview of reincarnation and karma, but beyond that, the moment they get into any of the details, there is no agreement. If you think otherwise, you haven't studied them very well. Each offers the "truth" of

a man or woman or a group. **It is their truth, not yours...
unless you care to accept it. TRUTH ONLY EXISTS AS
IT RELATES TO YOU.**

The Zen Master warns, "If you meet the Buddha on
the road, kill him." The meaning is that the only meaning
in life is what we bring to our own life. Any philosophy,
technique or truth that another might share with you is
an empty ideal unless it relates to you. "To kill the
Buddha" means to destroy the hope that anyone outside
yourself could be your master.

From another perspective, when you tell your truth,
when you are straight and honest with other people, you
will not tie up energy in unproductive, unpleasant ways.
Telling the truth releases you; it sets you free.

If you lie and hide something, it takes a lot of energy to
retain the lie. You always cover for it and "Babbler," that
notorious windbag that chatters incessantly in the back of
your mind, always remembers the lie and dwells upon it.
This sort of programming of your computer is self-
destructive in many ways.

Truth also directly relates to your **awareness.**
Awareness amounts to **how much you let yourself know
of your own truth.** Many of your truths remain buried in
the memory banks of your subconscious. The subconscious may contain knowledge, forgotten understanding,
talents or abilities, but it will also contain those events of
which you are ashamed, feel guilty or fearful. You do not
consciously know about them, so you lack that awareness, while at the same time, you experience the
programming effects.

PROBLEM/OPPORTUNITY

Some people see their problems as PROBLEMS! They
whine and worry and verbalize them over and over as the
soap operas of their lives. The more they repeat them, the

more they program the negative reality into their computer, resulting in compounded problems.

Others see their problems as opportunities. They use them as the basis of learning or reverse them into positive opportunity situations. Thus the resulting computer programming is only positive, begetting future positive potentials.

The only difference between problem-oriented people and opportunity-oriented people is **attitude** ... and it makes **all** the difference. Obviously, if you see your problems only as opportunities, you will no longer have any problems.

Extensive research testing has shown that 15 percent of success is attributable to talent, IQ or ability, and 85 percent of success is attributable to **attitude.** Attitude is the difference between the high achievers in life and all others.

NOW

We exist NOW and NOW is all that is. Now is outside of time. There is no past in which you were incomplete and there will never be a future in which you will become incomplete. Until you accept that you can only exist **NOW,** you will believe that fulfillment awaits you in an illusory future if you take the proper actions. This belief destroys the experience of **NOW** and you continually live in illusion.

This very moment is it. Nothing is hidden. All of your calculating and hoping and planning about how it will be someday ... all your dreams and plans ... THIS IS HOW IT ALL TURNED OUT. This is all there is. You've been planning all your life for the future, but you will never be aware of the future in the future ... you will only be aware of it in the **NOW.** We do not exist in time. We exist in self.

A Master of Life uses the time component, but he never accepts it as a reality that entraps him in actions to achieve fulfillment in an illusory future. He is always, at this moment, fulfilled, perfect, at peace and in balance.

DO WHAT YOU DO WHEN YOU DO IT

There is a Zen story about a man who stayed for a while in a small temple. He got up at 4:30 AM every day to clean the temple, but the monks all remained in bed until 7:00 or 8:00 AM. He cursed them as he swept, and despised them as he washed the floor. He hoped that the Master would get up and catch them slacking, but it never happened. The Master was in bed himself. The man judged the monks to be indifferent to their duties. He thought of nothing but their idleness and begrudged both his own labor and their slumbers.

Upon hearing of this, the Master asked "For whose sake do you clean the temple?" Then he answered it himself. "For your own sake. When you work, work for yourself, not for other people."

If you want your life to work better, when you work, just work; don't worry about whether others are working, or whether the temple will be burned down next week or not. When you write a book, don't worry about whether it will ever be published or whether anyone will ever read it. Everything that we do in life, directly or indirectly, we do for ourselves.

We get in the way of experiencing our lives. All we have is this moment. **NOW.** That's it. You can't touch the past or the future. All that exists is this moment and we seem incapable of enjoying it. When we make love we fantasize about making love to someone else or we recall some past episode, making it impossible to fully experience the moment. We plan something and have great fantasies about how it is going to be. Then when reality doesn't align with our preconceived ideas, we don't enjoy the situation, for we are attempting to mentally manipulate it.

39

Unless you can fully experience the moment, enjoying what you are experiencing for what it is, then you are not living your life. You are simply wandering through your fantasies and probably experiencing a good deal of anxiety as you trod along. Do what you do when you do it! See what a phenomenal difference it makes in the way you experience what you are doing. At your next meal, don't carry on a conversation and eat. Simply eat. **Feel** what it feels like to chew the food. **Taste** what the food really tastes like instead of gulping it down and rushing the next forkful to your mouth. It could be that you will **experience** eating for the first time in your life. Then relate the concept to other areas of your life and you may find that you are **experiencing** your life for the first time. Wisdom grows out of experience.

*The most that you
can give
to another
human being*

*Is to be all of
who you are.*

THE BASIC HUMAN RIGHTS

The basic human rights allow for expression as opposed to repression. A Master of Life grants them to all others while demanding them for himself.

1.

**IT IS YOUR RIGHT
TO DO ANYTHING
AS LONG AS YOU DO
NOT PURPOSELY HURT
SOMEONE ELSE
AND YOU ARE WILLING
TO ACCEPT
THE CONSEQUENCES.**

This ancient axiom is considered by many to be the one commandment. You were born free, you are free and only fear or value judgments will keep you from exercising this right.

2.

**IT IS YOUR RIGHT
TO MAINTAIN YOUR SELF-RESPECT
BY ANSWERING HONESTLY EVEN
IF IT DOES HURT SOMEONE ELSE,
AS LONG AS YOU ARE BEING
ASSERTIVE OPPOSED TO AGGRESSIVE.**

For a moment, imagine yourself in the following situation:

Your mother: "I have a big dinner planned for the entire family this Sunday, so you, John, and the children come over about one."

You: "We can't do that, Mother. We are going to rent a cabin in the woods this weekend."

Mother: "Well, I have this all planned. You can rent the cabin another weekend."

You: "We could rent the cabin another weekend, but I want to go this weekend."

Mother: "You mean you'd rather go to an old cabin in the woods than make your mother happy by coming over to her house for dinner?"

You: "This weekend I would rather go to the woods. Another weekend I might prefer to have dinner with you, Mother."

All right, your mother is now hurt because she put herself in a "choose between me and something else" contest, and you chose something else. It was a manipulative attempt to use guilt. You handled it in a kind way, even offering the compromise of coming for dinner on another weekend, so you have nothing to feel bad about. If your mother feels bad, it is her own doing and she will simply have to learn that you aren't going to fall for her old tricks anymore.

The key words on this particular right are "self-respect." A phony excuse or an unfelt apology will cause you to lose your self-respect and that is never acceptable.

3.

IT IS YOUR RIGHT TO
BE WHAT YOU ARE
WITHOUT CHANGING YOUR IDEAS
OR BEHAVIOR
TO SATISFY SOMEONE ELSE.

No one can change another person, nor should he expect another person to become anything other than what that person is. This is faulty thinking, for it is impossible to successfully repress anything. Any forced change will not last or will result in new eruptions of unsatisfactory behavior. Do you predicate your behavior on what another person wants you to be? Of course not. So how can you expect that person to change for you? We are all free human beings and should be respected for what we are, not for what someone else wants us to be. If your behavior makes another person uncomfortable, he or she has the right to leave. The same goes for you.

If you decide to remain in his environment, and since you realize that you couldn't change him if you wanted to, doesn't it make sense to accept him as he is? Basic, simple logic. Now, if you accept him as he is, then he is perfect from your perspective. You can't accept him and not accept him at the same time. Also, you need to respect him for what he is. That doesn't mean to respect him on a comparison scale with others, for that would be your evaluation, your judgment of how you want him to be. That's not it. You simply respect that he is what he is.

Now, if you can accept another as being perfect **the way he is** and you respect him for **what he is,** you must give up all your anger, hostility and blame for that person. This will naturally result from your realization that you had no right to feel the negative emotions in the first place.

4.

IT IS YOUR RIGHT
TO STRIVE
FOR SELF-ACTUALIZATION
(TO BECOME A MASTER OF LIFE).

You have the right to become all that you are capable of being in all areas of your life.

5.

IT IS YOUR RIGHT
TO USE YOUR OWN JUDGMENT
AS TO THE NEED PRIORITIES
OF YOURSELF AND OTHERS
IF YOU DECIDE TO ACCEPT ANY
RESPONSIBILITY FOR ANOTHER'S PROBLEM.

Ask your mate, children, parents, in-laws and friends what they feel your priorities should be and I'm sure you'll get many different answers. No one else can relate to your position and know what is best for you or what you should do. It is your value judgment as to what you will do with your time and in what order you choose to accomplish your tasks. It is also your right to choose whether or not to accept any responsibility for another's problem.

6.
IT IS YOUR RIGHT
NOT TO BE SUBJECTED
TO NEGATIVITY.

Negativity programs your computer in the wrong way and thus is very detrimental to you. The long-term effects of negative programming amount to a more negative life for you. Now combine that knowledge with the fact that humoring people and listening to their "soap operas" doesn't help them. From a programming perspective, it is equally detrimental to them. People can only help themselves when and if they are ready. Many are never ready. They thrive on the attention they get because of their problems. If that's their game, let them play it by themselves.

7.

IT IS YOUR RIGHT
TO OFFER NO EXCUSES OR JUSTIFICATIONS
FOR YOUR
DECISIONS OR BEHAVIOR.

You may want to explain why you feel or act a certain way to those with whom you share a close relationship, but it is your right not to. In interacting with people who are not close to you personally, explanations and excuses weaken your statements and position.

We all find ourselves in positions in which others imply that we owe them an explanation. Most of us are so well-trained that we react automatically and comply with their wishes without thinking. Also, all too often we explain ourselves even when no one has asked "why?"

8.

IT IS YOUR RIGHT
NOT TO CARE.

Life is filled with "you shoulds." You should improve yourself. You should care about the charity operation in your city. You should care about banning the bomb and ecology and pollution and planned parenthood and Aunt Nellie's broken leg. Your mother is getting old and is worrying about it so she thinks you should be concerned about old people in general. The PTA thinks you should attend monthly meetings and the FCC wants you to be concerned about violence on television. Your husband thinks you should roll his socks in pairs instead of just dumping them all in a heap in the dresser drawer. There are so many "you shoulds" that if "you did," you'd have no time left for anything else. DON'T "SHOULD" ON YOURSELF. You, and you alone, decide what to care about.

9.

IT IS YOUR RIGHT
TO BE
ILLOGICAL.

Logic usually works well in science, but it is never very predictable in human relationships and coping with people's desires, motivations and feelings. It is implied that logic indicates superior judgment but between two people, more often than not, it is simply used as a manipulative ploy.

As an example, your wife responds to your suggestion that you go to a movie this evening with: "We can't go to a movie tonight because we have to get up early tomorrow." That sounds logical, but from your perspective, missing an hour of sleep won't stop you from getting up early.

10.

IT IS YOUR RIGHT
TO CHANGE YOUR MIND.

People simply change their minds, and thank goodness they do. Otherwise, we would be a very rigid society and all the men would still be wearing crew cuts. What works for us today may not work tomorrow. What you liked last year may not fit with the more aware you of today. Or maybe you just got tired of living that lifestyle and changed. Changing your mind is healthy and normal, but other people may resist by challenging your right to do so. They will want explanations and the admission that your first choice was a mistake. "How can you change your mind after you committed yourself? You're irresponsible and will probably make a faulty decision next time."

You must be aware of their limited viewpoint and let their communications flow past you without affecting you.

11.

IT IS YOUR RIGHT
TO DEFEND YOURSELF.

Obviously, it is your right to defend yourself from any threat of physical violence. If the threat is verbal, however, it might be wise to hold back in your immediate response until you see whether what you're defending is your need to be right. In that case, you may get to be right ...and lose the game. You always have the right to respond to verbal aggression with assertiveness techniques.

3.
DIALOGUES

The following verbal exchanges are from tape recordings of dialogues between myself and the individual participants at **Bushido®** and **Master of Life®** seminars. After short talks or altered-state-of-consciousness processing sessions, the trainees are asked to share, question or interact if they desire to do so. At this time, they can request a microphone and verbally exchange concepts with me. My responses are primarily derived from the understanding previously communicated in this book.

Through this sharing, the trainees attain additional awareness. To achieve transformation, we must know our True Self. What is, is what you are. Not what you would like to be. Not your ideals. Wisdom can only result through understanding what is, for you can't change what you don't recognize. You may think you are loving and compassionate when what you really are is a cruel, spiteful person. Until you recognize your personality traits, you cannot make the changes that will allow your life to work better.

In the beginning of every Bushido Seminar, I explain, "I care far too much about each and every one of you to use our time together in an attempt to win friends or get your approval. I have only one goal here: To create the space for you to help yourself by finding your own truths, and I will do whatever is necessary to accomplish this, even at the cost of incurring your dislike."

1.

Trainee: "All this talk of fear in relationship to people confuses me. I can't stand my brother-in-law. I mean, I dread the idea of his coming over to visit, but I certainly don't fear him. I just can't stand the way he intrudes on our privacy and wastes our time."

Dick: "Obviously, you're resisting your brother-in-law, thus you often draw him into your life."

Trainee: "Yes."

Dick: "And fear is definitely involved in your relationship with your brother-in-law. The reason you hate to have him over is that you can't cope with him. The one fear, remember, is your inability to cope. As soon as you are honest and direct with your brother-in-law, you'll no longer dread his appearance. Then you can cope with him and thus there will be no fear."

Trainee: "That's it? Just speak up? But I don't think I can be that direct—I'd be afraid of hurting his feelings and totally ending a family relationship."

Dick: "If someone can't accept you as you really are, without oppressing you, do you really need that person in your life? I doubt it would be the end of your relationship, but if it was, that would mean your brother-in-law writes off those people he can't manipulate. Where does your self-respect come in?"

Trainee: "How could I possibly say it to him?"

Dick: "Directly, just the way you feel it, but without any resentment or hostility."

2.

Trainee: "I can't accept what you just said to her. You should never hurt anyone's feelings."

Dick: "There is no way you could possibly hurt anyone's feelings. They can only hurt their own feelings. It isn't what she says to him that will hurt him, only what he thinks about what she says to him."

Trainee: "Well, I can't see that repressing things is wrong. I work as a high school teacher and if I told the parents what I really think about their little darlings, I'd probably be fired."

Dick: "If repressing things is right for you, then fine. That's what you do. I don't tell anyone what to do. I simply want you to be aware of the results. Remember that I explained how it is impossible to repress anything; it will just come out in another way. You might release the pent-up anxiety at your husband. Maybe you really hold it in and get an ulcer, skin rash or some other physical disorder. Cancer might even result from long-term repression. Repression is fear ... fear is negative programming and you understand how programming works, so you know that you have to be creating a negative reality on down the line."

Trainee: "Oh, my God! It's awful that it works that way!"

Dick: "You feel that being direct and honest, being yourself with other human beings, is awful? The greatest gift you can give to another person is to be **all** of who you are."

Trainee: "Well ... I think I've got a lot of thinking to do."

3.

Trainee: "I just can't see any reason for the rules in this seminar."

Dick: "All right, I acknowledge that Kathy doesn't like the rules."

Trainee: "All right, what?! The rules are stupid and I think you get off on enforcing them."

Dick: "That's your conclusion, Kathy. I can't argue with your conclusion."

Trainee: "Well, it is time to let up on the rules."

Dick: "The rules are what is, Kathy. They will remain exactly as they have been established. You can resist them if you want, but that doesn't change them. You can make your life difficult by resisting the rules or you can relax and accept that what is, is. Be aware that I don't care how you handle it."

Trainee: "There are plenty of things in life that need to be resisted. Thank God some people resist them."

Dick: "Resist what you can do something about, Kathy, and stop resisting what you can't change. Gravity exists. You can resist it if you want, but it won't do you much good. The high price of gasoline is a reality, but if you want to resist it and curse and swear and fight back, fine, go ahead. From my perspective, you are making your life unnecessarily difficult. The rules of this seminar exist, and whether you like it or not, they will continue to exist. You see, Kathy, you are a resister. That's what Kathy does. This training room is a mirror of your life and you resist your life."

Trainee: "Oh, come on, that's bullshit! I don't resist my life, I just resist dumb, unnecessary rules."

Dick: "Are you married, Kathy?"

Trainee: "I'm in the process of a divorce."

Dick: "He wasn't the type of husband you wanted him to be, huh?"

Trainee: "He certainly wasn't."

Dick: "And isn't that resistance, Kathy? You certainly resisted his being what he was. Did you tell him how you wanted him to be?"

Trainee: "I did, and there was no way he was going to change."

Dick: "You resist your job, too, don't you, Kathy?"

Trainee: "I quit. It was a family job and no one in their right mind would remain in a zoo like that."

Dick: "Yet the rest of the family seems to handle it fine. Kathy thinks it's a zoo because the job isn't exactly the way she wants it to be, and the other employees aren't the way she wants them to be. Did you tell them how to get it together, Kathy?"

Trainee: "Yes, and if they followed my advice, the whole company would be a lot more profitable."

Dick: "And Kathy doesn't resist anything? Kathy, you are so full of it that you can't even see that you are making your life miserable by resisting your life."

Trainee: "My life isn't miserable."

Dick: "Bullshit! The reason you're standing here going through this with me is that you desperately want to get rid of the constant mental pain you feel. Do you want to get rid of it, Kathy? Are you really ready to find out why you do what you do and get rid of it, or are you going to stand there and continue to run your 'little brat' number?"

Trainee: "I wish the pain would go away."

Dick: "All right, Kathy. Center yourself." [a technique Bushido students are taught] "Somewhere in your background is a primary reason for the resistance you exert toward the people and situations in your life. We are going to go back to the cause of this resistance. I will count from one to three and on the count of three, vivid impressions will come into your mind. One, two, three. Trust what comes in."

Trainee: "They have no right! They have no right to do this to us! Who do they think they are?" (She is screaming and crying.) "We're people—they can't **do** this to us!"

Dick: "Where are you, Kathy? I want to know where you are and what is happening."

Trainee: "Auschwitz. They're ... they're treating us like cattle. They're ... oh, God ..." [Magnitude 1 Experience]

Dick: "Go ahead and experience how awful it is.

Totally experience your resentment and how miserable and shitty it is. EXPERIENCE IT."

Trainee: "It's awful ... it's awful!" (more crying and sobbing)

Dick: "Experience it!" (two or three minutes pass) "How is it now?"

Trainee: "It feels better." (long pause) "It really does feel better!"

Dick: "All right, let go of the impressions, and if you want to totally let go of the past, you will forgive the people who did this to you. For some reason, you needed to experience this situation, but it has caused you to resist your marriage, your job, various forms of authority, the rules of this training ... and what you were really resisting was being a Jewish prisoner in a German concentration camp. That doesn't relate anymore, Kathy, unless you want it to. If you want to continue to make your life miserable, that is your choice, but at least understand the real reasons behind your attitude and actions. Can you forgive them, Kathy?"

Trainee: "I forgive them. Oh, God, I FORGIVE THEM! I FORGIVE THEM!"

4.

Trainee: "This Master of Life awareness sounds great in theory, but I think you'd have to be superhuman to put it into practice when you live with someone as negative as my husband."

Dick: "Do you want to remain in the marriage, Sheila?"

Trainee: "Yes, I'm not saying I don't love him, I'm just saying he is extremely negative and sometimes very difficult to tolerate."

Dick: "Well, Sheila, I contend that your husband is acceptable just the way he is, and it is **you** who has the problem. Sometimes the only way to be responsible to yourself is to remove yourself from the environment you find yourself in. But since you want to remain married, the only way to handle your problem is to totally experience it or change your viewpoint. It isn't your husband that's affecting you, it's **your** reactions to what he says and does. He doesn't make you react that way. You do it all on your own, responding from your viewpoint that he shouldn't be the way he is. You want him to change and be the way you want him to be!"

Trainee: "Yes, I'd like him to change, but I know that's never going to happen. I still can't help being upset by him."

Dick: "Wrong. You can stop being upset by him once you fully accept the futility of the upsets. Right now, you're playing the part of the victim and I think you're still expecting him to see the light and change. But people don't change unless they really want to change for themselves."

Trainee: "Well, Frank certainly doesn't want to change for himself. I guess you're right. I think I am still expecting him to see the error in his ways. Dumb, huh?"

Dick: "Probably, Sheila. If you are going to remain married, you need to accept that you, and you alone, are the cause of the unhappiness in your marriage. What is, is that Frank is negative and difficult to tolerate. You need to accept this reality and stop reacting to him. Get that it is Frank's right to be negative and it is your right **not to be affected.** That's conscious detachment. And when you are no longer affected by a problem, you no longer have a problem, even though nothing about the problem situation may have changed. The only thing that has changed is your viewpoint. You have accepted that what is, is, and thus transformed the way you experience a portion of your life. Can you get that, Sheila?"

Trainee: "Sounds like I have everything to gain and nothing to lose by working on it."

5.

Dick: "We all have soap operas, stories that we repeat and repeat in one form or another until we can verbalize them without thinking. They are our tapes which we play at every opportunity: 'As The World Rotates ... sponsored by Tide soap, and starring ... YOU!'

"Here are some examples: 'I'm underpaid and unappreciated.' 'I know how to run the company better than my boss!' 'My astrology is screwed up because my Aries doesn't line up with my husband's Capricorn.' 'I've got bad karma.' 'My husband never takes me anywhere.' 'My wife never gives me enough sex.' 'My husband always wants sex.' 'My wife doesn't understand me.' 'It's my lot in life—my parents never had any money, so I'll never have any money either.' 'My hemorrhoids are acting up again.'

"Those close to you know your soap operas. They've heard them often enough that they could probably repeat them word for word, just as you could repeat theirs. Think about this for a few minutes. Everyone close your eyes and answer a few questions as I ask them: What is your primary soap opera, your number one gripe or complaint?" (pause) "When does this soap opera get aired, and who is your primary audience? Your mate, your friends, co-workers, relatives, strangers, your kids?" (pause) "All right. Now I want you to become fully aware that every time you repeat your soap opera to others, you program it into your subconscious mind and increase the effect of the problem on you."

****

Trainee: "All right. I get that my soap opera is my constant complaining about my husband: He isn't considerate, he doesn't seem to enjoy being with me ... he just doesn't act like a loving husband should act. Am I supposed to ignore the way he is?"

Dick: "There is no way to ignore what is, Barbara. What you need to realize is that your constant complaining about your relationship is actually programming the negative aspects of your relationship.

"Verbally repeat an idea and you program that concept into your reality. I know a woman whose soap opera is, 'I was raped as a young girl and it has ruined all my relationships with men.' Guess who has been raped several times since and has yet to experience a long-term, fulfilling relationship with a man?"

Trainee: "Do you mean that when I talk with my girlfriends about Roger, I am actually causing him to be that way? I can't buy that."

Dick: "When you complain about your husband, you create an internal image of a negative relationship. Your subconscious accepts all such input as programming and works to bring the situation into reality."

Trainee: "Okay, I guess I didn't put that together. But I don't see that there is any hope. When Roger and I were going together, everything was beautiful. Then we got married and within six months, things were miserable. He started ordering me around and acting like a little Hitler, becoming more and more dictatorial. Eventually, I accepted that and went along with him and our relationship smoothed out a lot, but there is no consideration or caring on his part."

Dick: "All right, Barbara, let's find out why your relationship is the way it is. We are now going to work together to further your understanding. Somewhere in your past, in this or a previous lifetime, something happened to cause your present relationship problems. I want you to go backward in time to the beginning of this situation." (induction given) "All right, speak up and tell me what you sense or see ... what is happening?"

Trainee: "I'm on a ship, an old sailing ship. I'm a man and

I'm dirty . . . really dirty. The . . . oh, the captain is yelling at me. I'm the first mate. I'm picking up the cat-o'-nine-tails as they tie a man to the mast. I'm whipping him, whipping him really hard. I seem to be enjoying it." (long pause) "I get it now. I am enjoying it because I don't like the man I'm whipping. We've fought before and this is a chance to get in some extra whacks. He knows it, too."

Dick: "What did the man do?"

Trainee: "Nothing to do with me this time. He took something out of the hold. Food. He sneaked extra food."

Dick: "And who is that man in your current life?"

Trainee: "Oh, God, I think he is my husband. Yes, I'm sure of it."

Dick: "All right. I now want you to recall the situation and the room and open your eyes on the count of three. One, two, three."

Trainee: "An eye for an eye, huh? This time I've got to let him mentally whip me to make up for it?"

Dick: "Don't assume that you've experienced the whole background for there were causes that created the effects that you just observed and before that, other causes. I just want you to see that the two of you have created your current situation as an opportunity to rise above past fear programming. You need to be aware of all the facts, or as many as possible, before you begin to work out a solution.

"Let's go back and examine some additional concepts that are working against you. You are making a giant mistake in expecting your husband to be the way you want him to be. You are resisting what is and it is causing you suffering. You want him to be considerate and enjoy being with you."

Trainee: "Like Sheila, am I supposed to accept that my husband is a son of a bitch?"

Dick: "Is he a son of a bitch?"

Trainee: "Yes."

Dick: "Have you been able to change him up until now?"

Trainee: "No."

Dick: "Of course not. Get that you will never be able to change him. He might decide to change on his own. I doubt it, and he might. He is a son of a bitch. That's what is. It is your resistance to his being an S.O.B. that is causing your greatest anxiety."

Trainee: "Well, what should I do?"

Dick: "It is your relationship, Barbara. I don't have your answers. I can only suggest that if you decide to remain with Roger, your life will be a little less difficult if you accept what is."

Trainee: "Great!"

Dick: "Let's take it a little farther. You let Roger tell you what to do and you're taking it? Resenting it—'stuffing it,' as we say—smiling on the outside and keeping the anger inside."

Trainee: "That's about it. At least we don't fight this way."

Dick: "There is absolutely no way to repress your feelings totally, Barbara. It will come out in some way or another. Maybe you take out your frustrations on someone else, like your kids or fellow workers, or maybe you allow it to manifest as a physical problem."

Trainee: "Like migraine headaches?"

Dick: "Are you speaking from experience?"

Trainee: "Yes. They started shortly after we were married and now I get a migraine at least once a week. They're killers."

Dick: "Okay. This is the result of forcing change on someone else, Barbara. Roger has forced you to change, to be other than what you are. Outwardly, you have cooperated while inwardly you are resisting it. We all have to let others be what they are. If we don't like it then we have the freedom to leave and they have the same right. You and Roger have a problem that I hope you can turn into an opportunity. Ideally, you will find a solution and rise above your past negativity."

Trainee: "Where do I start?"

Dick: "Where do you start, Barbara?"

Trainee: "My own answers, right? Okay, first, no more soap operas ... they just program me downhill. Then I guess I'm just going to have to be straight with him. We're going to talk and there will have to be some kind of compromise."

Dick: "Sounds like a good start."

6.

Trainee: "I just want to fall out of love with my husband, then maybe I'll be able to let go of the ridiculous situation we share. All we do is hurt each other, but we still love each other. I want to fall out of love."

Dick: "What does love have to do with marriage? Most love is fear: jealousy, possessiveness, envy, frustration, anxiety. That's not love. You assume that you have to be in love to be married; in reality, for the vast majority of people, love has nothing to do with it. But get that the more you resist each other, the more intensely you are involved with each other. It may be negative involvement but it is still involvement and this is what you both need. As long as you struggle against something, you're locked into it and you perpetuate its influence on your life. When you fight with each other, at least you know he cares about what you are doing or saying. Otherwise he wouldn't bother to react. We're back to fear and the law of resistance again. The next session we'll be conducting may provide you with valuable insights as to how you might approach your situation."

Trainee: "I'm really not happy with the way I am and I'm going to try to change."

Dick: "Don't do that. Trying is lying. There is no such thing as trying. When someone says, 'I'll try,' what they're really saying is, 'I won't do it now.' For years I've demonstrated it this way: Take a pencil and hold it between your index finger and your thumb. Now start thinking, 'I'm trying to drop it, I'm trying to drop it, I'm trying to drop it,' over and over and don't let any other thought come into your mind. And try to drop it while you're doing that."

Trainee: "I can't drop it."

Dick: "Right. Trying blocks doing. Trying is an excuse. Don't try to do it! Just DO IT. You either get results or you have excuses why you don't. It's time to drop the excuses and get results."

*N*othing is impossible
to a willing mind.

Books of Han Dynasty

8.

Trainee: "I'm afraid I'm just not clear on exactly what you mean by transformation, by transforming the way you experience your life."

Dick: "Transformation literally means to rise above or go beyond the limits ordinarily imposed by form. Transformation or self-actualization is a means of housing a different essence in the same form. If I could change a peach into a pear, that wouldn't be transformation. If I could take a peach and turn it into a peach that *tasted* like like a pear, that would be transformation. To a person who has experienced transformation, the world remains exactly as it was before. The immediate circumstances of their existence are the same. What has changed is their viewpoint of those circumstances, the way they relate to their world. The circumstances haven't changed at all."

Trainee: "Okay, that helps me get it, but I'm looking for some real changes."

Dick: "When you transform your viewpoint, you rise above the problem. The situation is the same, yet you've stopped resisting it. Thus what often happens is the problem situation resolves itself."

9.

Trainee: "I just can't buy that what is, is. You always say, 'Create your own reality.' That's a paradox."

Dick: "I say to change what you can change and accept what you can't change **if** you're going to remain in the environment. Don't waste energy on what you can't change. When asked about the meaning of life, Zen Master Joshu answered, 'What's hot is hot and what's cold is cold.' That's what is."

Trainee: "Well, my husband is a bastard, and I'm going to change him if it kills me!"

Dick: "If it kills you! Interesting choice of words, Susan. Can't you get that when you seek to change, criticize or reject someone else, you are experiencing fear and that fear is within you. It is your fear of coping with the situation."

Trainee: "No way! I just want him to stop being such a bastard."

Dick: "Susan, your husband is a bastard. That's what is. You can accept it or you can fight it, and regardless of what you do, it won't change what is: He is a bastard."

Trainee: "What if I tell him if he doesn't change, I'm going to leave?"

Dick: "You can always do that, Susan. He might even change. He might repress what he really is and successfully stuff it for a while, but I can guarantee you that it'll come out in some other way. It will come out. Maybe he'll cheat on you instead, or maybe he'll actually behave himself and become a martyr with an ulcer. Martyrs create problems for other people. They are guaranteed pains in the neck."

Trainee: "Well, I could always use programming powers to change him."

Dick: "Susan, get that the problem is within you, not in your husband. If you use programming to manipulate someone else, it will always backfire. It is time to accept what is, Susan, and experience your problem."

Trainee: "Experience it?"

Dick: "Yes, totally **experience** it. Ignoring your problem or attempting to live with it are both forms of resistance. The more you resist it in your mind, the more it seems to build up into a resentment. Totally experience the resentment you feel toward your husband. Take time to be quiet and then get into it. Feel how miserable it feels, examine every facet of how you are affected and just experience the resentment."

Trainee: "Then what?"

that most of the resentment is gone. Total experience can eliminate many problems."

Trainee: "And what if that doesn't work?"

Dick: "We approach change from four different perspectives in this training, as you already know. Yet each way is a matter of you changing yourself. Never expect others to change for you."

10.

Trainee: "You say to totally experience the problem. Well, I'm trapped in a miserable marriage and I don't intend to sit around experiencing in my mind in an attempt to override what I know is a miserable situation."

Dick: "If it is so lousy, why are you still married, Sam?"

Trainee: "For the life of me, I don't know."

Dick: "When you totally experience your emotions, you're going to discover things about how you really feel; you may find that things aren't as bad as you perceived them to be or you may experience what it is that is blocking you from leaving. If that is the case, once you experience the block, you may leave. Regardless of how it works out, your problem of experiencing yourself as trapped in a miserable marriage will disappear."

Simplicity is the secret to well-being.

Trainee: "I see these concepts as being rather selfish."

Dick: "I hope so."

Trainee: "Well, that's awful."

Dick: "Laura, we all need to know the facts before attempting to deal with things. Can you accept that?"

Trainee: "Yes, but I don't see that there is any justification for selfishness."

Dick: "Laura, you've never been anything but selfish in your entire life. You always place your own interests before those of anyone else."

Trainee: "I do not! I help..."

Dick: "Yes, you do, Laura ... AND SO DOES EVERY OTHER PERSON ON THIS PLANET. Now, let's talk about reality. You always act in your own self-interest. That may not be the way you want to be, but that is what is. The individual who fools himself into believing that he is selfless and altruistic does so to hide from the fact that, deep inside, he feels his life is puny and meaningless. He claims to be selfless, and in so doing, he gains enormously in self-esteem. His vanity becomes boundless as he lets everyone else know all he has done to 'help'!

"Another point about self-sacrifice: Even when initiated for the most noble of causes, it produces a facility for hatred. Even if the cause is to save starving children, the altruist is very likely to be violently intolerant to those who do not agree with his priorities.

"You do have a choice of being rationally or irrationally selfish. The irrationally selfish person is what most of us think of when we cringe at the word 'selfish.' The guy who grabs everything for himself. The rationally selfish individual responds to the needs of others in order to obtain his own objectives. He is often a very 'giving' person, because he knows that you need to give in order to receive in human relationships.

"Let's look at a few examples so you can better understand this, Laura. Let's assume that you planned to go shopping with a girlfriend this Saturday. Your husband informs you on Friday evening that he has to work on a special office project on Saturday and asks that you help him. If you agree to help him, would you be putting his interests before yours, Laura?"

Trainee: "I certainly would be."

Dick: "No, you wouldn't. You would choose for your own self-interest, just as you always do. Maybe you want to avoid the confrontation that might ensue if you said no. Maybe you might need help yourself someday and don't want him to turn you down. Maybe you want to purchase a new outfit next week and feel he'd be more likely to think favorably of it if you help him out. Maybe you feel you owe it to him. Maybe you want to avoid potential guilt feelings that might result if you play while he works. Maybe you feel that a good wife should help her husband. In that case, you'd be doing it to live up to your own self-image of what a good wife should be. You wouldn't want to live with a negative self-image in that area. I don't know what your reasons would be, but whatever your decision, it would be in your own self-interest. Can you get that, Laura?"

Trainee: "Yes, I can see that, but there are other areas where people put the interest of others first. Take a situation I read about in the paper recently. A car turned over and a stranger risked his life to climb into the burning car and pull the injured driver out. How about that?"

Dick: "The man who risked his life did so because he would feel far better about himself, knowing that he had risked his life to save a stranger, than to live with the knowledge that someone died whom he might have been able to save."

Trainee: "What if your own child was in the burning car?"

Dick: "It would be the same situation, only now add the element of love and the knowledge that your child brings you great pleasure simply in his existence. There would be a much stronger sense of self-interest in risking your life for his."

Trainee: "All right, but you certainly can't claim that men like Albert Schweitzer and Mahatma Gandhi acted in their own self-interest."

Dick: "Of course I can. Gandhi supposedly sacrificed himself for freedom in the name of the East Indian people. Gandhi accepted what was going on politically at that time and chose to make millions of people happy. That was what he chose for his own fulfillment. Martyrs are among the most selfish of people. They have insatiable egos. It is only how people choose their own fulfillment that differs. Gandhi thought on a big scale—for his fulfillment, he needed to be a hero to millions."

12.

Trainee: "You're horrible. You've made everyone in this room feel horrible."

Dick: "Not everyone, yet this subject does seem to create considerable resistance, doesn't it? You can't stand facing a reality that isn't the way you want it to be. All I'm talking about is reality. Everyone in the world acts in their own self-interest at all times. So what? That's like saying gravity exists. Face the fact that gravity exists; that's what is. I'm not saying to stop assisting your fellow human being; I'm saying **stop fooling yourself about why you assist your fellow human being.** Stop playing the self-sacrificing martyr. To people who are aware, those who claim to be selfless are actually renouncing themselves.

"The most selfish people do great good. They are of service to the planet in many beautiful ways. I write books and conduct trainings that I feel free peoples' minds and this, in my view, is a service to the planet, yet I am not fooling myself about why I do it. I do it because I need to do it. If I didn't, I'd be unhappy. Thus, for my happiness, I write books. It's only how we achieve our individual happiness that differs.

"A friend of mine claims to have a deep social conscience. His life is a matter of assisting different causes, and in so doing, he experiences happiness and self-esteem. To be aware of the reason behind the effort does not diminish the results he achieves."

Trainee: "Why is this so hard for me to accept?"

Dick: "You've been conditioned all your life to accept a lot of fairy tales. You've been brainwashed. This training is about getting rid of old programming and creating a space where you can decide, based upon facts, what kind of personal reality you want to create. You're starting to see life with a transformed perspective. The situations in your life won't change at all at first, but the way you see them will have changed. Viewing reality as it is can be quite a shock."

*The less effort,
the faster
and more powerful
you will be.*

Bruce Lee

13.

Trainee: "I can't stand this. You're shooting down all our ideals."

Dick: "An ideal is a concept, John. Show me an ideal. Attempt to experience an ideal. You can't. An ideal is a belief that clouds reality. Peoples' lives don't work because they run around with their heads in the clouds, wanting things to be the way they want them to be instead of accepting reality as it is and using that as a basis for life."

Trainee: "My life works!"

Dick: "Does it really, John? This training is for people who want their lives to begin to work. Interesting that you're here when yours is already working so well. Is your marriage really happy and are you fulfilled in your career? Be straight, John!"

Trainee: "No, but I don't think anyone else experiences that either!"

Dick: "You just made my point, John. Your life doesn't work and neither do the lives of most people. By the way, there are plenty of people who do have extremely happy marriages and experience fulfillment in their careers. Let's get back to selflessness, John. I think that is what you got stuck on in the first place."

Trainee: "The minute I say anything, it sounds like I think my life is puny and meaningless. You set us up that way."

Dick: "What do you want to say, John?"

Trainee: "Sometimes I put the self-interest of others before my own. Period."

Dick: "There are three types of people, John. The first type is admittedly acting in his or her own self-interest. These are the only people I ever get close to personally, because in doing so, my life is always easier. The second type knows that he acts in his own self-interest but he attempts to make you believe otherwise. Type three doesn't get that he acts in his own self-interest or doesn't allow himself to be aware of his truth in the matter, thus he sincerely believes that he sometimes thinks of others first. Now you can believe what you want to believe, John, but you're going to go through life being disappointed and wondering why things don't work out better for you."

Trainee: "I still can't buy it."

Dick: "Give me an example, John, of how you put someone else's interests before your own."

Trainee: "My mother—she is very sickly and I take care of her because I love her; I really want to take care of her."

Dick: "John, let's look at it another way. How would you like to live with the idea that you are the sort of man who doesn't love his mother, who neglects her and hides from his responsibility to her in a time of need?"

Trainee: "I couldn't handle that! Who could?"

Dick: "Then can you get that you take care of your mother out of your own self-interest because you couldn't live with the idea of not taking care of her? The responsibility you feel for her is self-imposed and you are doing it for yourself."

Trainee: "I think I'm beginning to see what you mean."

Dick: "John, understand that I think it is beautiful that you take care of your mother. Just understand why you do it and don't be a martyr."

14.

Dick: "This training is about leaping into the unknown and finding your Self within. The True Self is found when the false one is renounced. When you function as your True Self, your life will work better. You can experience loving yourself for the first time, and then—and only then—will you sincerely be able to **love** others. You see, to experience loving yourself, you need to know who you are. Once you've got it together personally, you can

really be of service to others.

"Can you all get that being straight with yourself about acting in your own self-interest is part of renouncing your false self? Can you get that when you recognize your True Self, you can begin to make your voice and your efforts count in this universe? Can you get that self-interest is the only altruism that exists?"

Trainees: "Yes!!!" (in unison)

15.

Trainee: "No one in here has spoken up about affairs. It seems like that subject is being ignored. You've just destroyed everything I've accomplished in the last few months by talking about aliveness!" [an SST discussion and process about fully experiencing life]

Dick: "How did I do that, Betty?"

Trainee: "When you spoke about aliveness and these people shared their moments of ultimate aliveness, I felt awful. That's how I felt with the lover I just said goodbye to. I've been working to reestablish my relationship with my husband. Someone took pictures of my lover and me together and I had to make a choice or face a scandal. I chose my husband."

Dick: "And?"

Trainee: "Well, I love my husband, but I'm not **in love** with him. I didn't want a scandal that would have harmed my lover; I also have two children to consider. But when you talked about living your life with aliveness and when I see how you and your wife interact, I feel really sad. We felt the way the two of you obviously feel about each other."

Dick: "So you're a victim of other people's happiness? Do you believe that since we're happy, and Sam over there is happy, and since Carol, Donna, Bill and Gene are all happy that there isn't any left over for you?"

Trainee: "Well, I know there aren't any victims. I've gotten that out of this training. But it is too late to get my lover back. I can't leave my husband; I couldn't go through all the stuff with my friends and family again. They were all so happy that my husband and I are back together again, I couldn't let them down. But what am I going to do?"

Dick: "I don't know what you are going to do, but I'd ask you to reconsider basing your decisions on fear. What is the worst that could possibly happen as a result of this situation?"

Trainee: "I'd end up alone. Without anyone."

Dick: "What about that?"

Trainee: "I couldn't handle that. I really need to be in love. I have to be with someone."

Dick: "Betty, can't you see that these fear-based needs are programming your losses? Your relationships are based on avoiding losing, upon resisting, thus you are programming the loss."

Trainee: "Okay, I guess I see that because that's what is happening in my life. But I still don't know what to do! What should I do?"

Dick: "Betty, I don't have your answers. You are the one—the only one—who has your answers. There are certainly directions to be found in this training; you must decide if they are right for you. In your confusion, it is obvious that you are not clear on your intent. You don't really know what you want."

Trainee: "That's true. I don't. I want my lover but it's too late for that. Yet I don't know if I want him at the cost it would mean: scandal, harm to my kids and hurt for all my friends and family. I still want to be what a good wife should be yet my husband cut me out of his life long ago. He separated from me first. At the same time, I want to experience joy and growth like I did with my lover."

70

Dick: "Betty, listen to yourself! It's all fear! You have no clarity of intent. You're repressing your real feelings, which is self-destructive. It won't work for any extended period of time. You're more concerned with what others will think than with what you feel. Take some time to be alone and allow your own wisdom to come into your awareness. Ask yourself the right questions. Betty, ask yourself, 'What do I need to know? I know I have the answer within me and I'm willing to experience whatever I need to experience to know this.' The answers are there when we finally come up with the right questions.

"I get that you are looking for an easy answer. Obviously, there isn't one, is there? Nobody ever guaranteed you any easy answers. Yet there are probably more alternatives than you are aware of. There always are. When you decide what you want, and then start to be direct and honest, your life will get straight once again."

Trainee: "Thank you."

*Never say,
"I am right
and
you are wrong."*

Wisdom is provided

*to different people
at different times
in different ways.*

16.

Trainee: "I'd like to know where you think ego belongs in all of this. I'm attempting to suppress my ego to speed my spiritual evolution."

Dick: "To worry about your ego is the ultimate ego trip. Get off it. Your ego is what is. To attempt to get rid of your ego is to resist your ego; thus, you'll end up with more ego. Experience what you experience without repressing."

*Don't run away
from life,
run with it.
Freedom
comes through
total acceptance
of reality.*

17

Dick: "We have about 200 people in this training room and three-fourths of you are women. How many of you do not have a primary relationship in your life at this time?" (almost half the hands are raised) "How many of you really want to live alone?" (four hands are raised) "I don't believe the four of you. I've worked with thousands of people and have yet to find anyone who doesn't desire a warm, joyful, fulfilling relationship in which they can share experiences of mutual personal growth."

Trainee: "That's ridiculous. I've been married twice and I don't see any value in it. I enjoy sex and now I can sleep with any man I want to."

Dick: "When you said 'sex' just now, Linda, your body language became very anxious. What's going on with you and sex?"

Trainee: "Nothing. I love sex."

Dick: "Linda, you can play that game if you want to and hold onto your secret, or you can be open and honest and maybe find some answers of your own that will make your life work better."

Trainee: (voice choking as tears form in her eyes) "The only problem is that I pretend I'm having an orgasm when I'm not. I want the man to think he's a really great lover so he'll ... uh ..."

Dick: "So he'll like you better."

Trainee: "Yeah. Is that so bad?"

Dick: "It's not bad or good. It's only that it keeps you from experiencing sex."

Trainee: "Oh, really!"

Dick: "Yes, **really!** You've been far too busy wearing a mask and pretending to be something you aren't. To experience something is to be totally focused on what is transpiring. It's impossible to have an orgasm while worrying about what he thinks."

Trainee: (crying) "I can get off fine afterwards, or the next day on my own."

Dick: "Of course. When you masturbate, you totally experience it. There are no fears or expectations blocking the experience. What I'm getting is that you aren't relating completely to anyone and that you're aching inside to do so."

Trainee: (crying) "Well, it just never works out. Every time I get close to a man, it falls apart. It's just too much trouble."

Dick: "What's the payoff in keeping things the way they are, Linda? For some fear-based reason, you are creating this situation exactly the way it is."

Trainee: (angrily) "I don't know!"

Dick: "Oh, yes, you do. You have all your own answers. **Why do you want to be alone, Linda? Why do you want to be alone?**"

Trainee: (crying and sobbing) "So I won't have to pretend all the time!"

Dick: "All right now, let go of this." (putting his arms around her and holding her) "Do you understand that the reason you've avoided getting involved in a primary relationship isn't valid?"

Trainee: "Yes, I do see that. In fact, I really want a relationship, just not a painful one."

Dick: "Now, when I'm talking with Linda, I'm talking to every single person in this training room. Linda has been wearing a mask, pretending to be something she isn't. When we do that, it takes a great deal of energy, thus we're only able to wear the mask for limited periods of time. For Linda, wearing this mask is so draining that it's easier to be by herself than to be in a relationship. Because of this, she subconsciously destroys every potential relationship. Once Linda decides that it's okay to be direct and honest in her communications with the men in her life, she'll probably allow herself to be open to involvement in a relationship."

Trainee: "But I feel that I need to make the men feel good about themselves."

Dick: "I believe the greatest gift you can give to another human being is to be all of who you are. If you are yourself and totally experience your sexual involvements, you'll probably start enjoying sex again and the men will automatically feel good about your enjoyment. But let's just say for a moment that you pretend successfully and the man falls in love with you. Does he love you or the mask you're wearing, Linda?"

Trainee: "The mask, I guess."

Dick: "Of course. And one day the mask would become too heavy. You'd take it off and he'd scream about the fact that you'd changed; you weren't the girl he married."

Trainee: "Ohhh. That's exactly what happened in both my marriages."

Dick: "Linda, be yourself. Be just what you are and nothing else. That way, if love develops, it's based on the way you really are. If it doesn't, there aren't any illusions to be painfully dissolved later."

Do things that contribute to your awareness.

Refrain from things which do not.

18.

Trainee: "I really want to establish a good relationship with a man. I've been career oriented, but I'm ready to share my life. I'd like to get married. I date several times a week. The problem is, I just can't find the right man. I'm in a position to meet many men who are eligible, and I've had many who want to get serious, but they all have flaws I couldn't live with."

Dick: "Describe the ideal man for me, Diana."

Trainee: "Well, he would be good-looking, at least six feet tall. Preferably blond. I can't stand men who are overweight. He would have a lucrative, well-established career and be a responsible person. I also want someone who is morally adult. Since we're talking about ideal, I guess I should add that I'd like him to be kind of a 'white knight.'"

Dick: "What does 'responsible' mean?"

Trainee: "He fulfills his obligations, does what he says he'll do and has a good credit rating, which at least proves some sort of responsibility."

Dick: "What does 'morally adult' mean?"

Trainee: "Someone who doesn't have any kinky ideas and is satisfied with one woman. Someone I could count on not to have affairs."

Dick: "'Kinky ideas'?"

Trainee: "You know! Weird sex! Half the men I've met are open to threesomes ... women with women ... or other weird ideas. Some of them think it is more creative to make love on the kitchen table than the normal way."

Dick: "Normal way?"

Trainee: "Normal sex in bed. Regular positions. I don't want to keep on this."

Dick: "Why not?"

Trainee: "It seems to me that you're getting too personal, looking for perverse details."

Dick: "Does the subject of sex make you uncomfortable, Diana?"

Trainee: "I don't think it needs to be discussed! The whole world is obsessed with it."

Dick: "Okay, just a couple more questions about sex. How often would the ideal man make love to you?"

Trainee: "Once or twice a week."

Dick: "Would you look forward to those times or would you be complying for the sake of the man?"

Trainee: "It would be all right because I know men need sex."

Dick: "Don't women need sex?"

Trainee: "Some seem to more than others. But if they were fulfilled in other ways, I doubt that they would."

Dick: "By 'fulfilled in other ways,' do you mean, for example, having a successful career?"

Trainee: "Sure."

Dick: "I have one more question about your ideal man. What do you mean by 'white knight'?"

Trainee: "A man who would kind of sweep me off my feet with flowers and romance. He'd make the important decisions and carry me off into his world."

Dick: "Do you know anyone who lives up to your image of an ideal man? Anyone, anywhere, married or not?"

Trainee: (silent for a while, thinking) "No, I guess I don't."

Dick: "What if you found a man who fulfilled your image of the ideal man in every way except for an occasional desire to have sex on the kitchen table or experiment with anal sex?"

Trainee: (frowns and shakes her head) "No."

Dick: "What if he were ideal in every way except that he was 20 pounds overweight?"

Trainee: "I can't stand men who are overweight."

Dick: "Okay, Diana. Let's assume you found the ideal man and the two of you fall in love and get married. Now, what would the cost be to you? For everything you want, there is a price to pay in either time, money, effort or sacrifice. What would you have to give up?"

Trainee: (thinks hard for several seconds) "My freedom to come and go as I please. I'd have to respond sexually. I'd certainly have more responsibilities. I know I'd have to compromise in areas such as food, entertainment, friends, social events, vacations ... just about everything, I guess."

Dick: "Freedom, sex, responsibilities, compromise ... how would you really feel about making those adjustments, Diana? Be straight."

Trainee: "Not real good, to be perfectly honest. Almost sounds like it's more trouble than it's worth, doesn't it?"

Dick: "Does it, Diana?"

Trainee: "Yes, it does, when I think about it."

Dick: "And, you're getting clear that you really don't want a relationship, aren't you? You have no **clarity of intent,** there are too many **negative payoffs** in keeping your life exactly the way it is. You have unrealistic **expectations** and are obviously filled with **fear** in regard to establishing a relationship."

Trainee: "But I do. I really do. I would love to be married like all my girlfriends are; something inside me is almost obsessed with the idea ..." (crying) "A girl my age **should** be married."

Dick: " 'Should be married'? You're 'shoulding' on yourself! Who says so? Where is that written?"

Trainee: "All my girlfriends are ..." (sobbing)

Dick: (putting a hand on her shoulder) "All right, Diana, let go of this. I realize this is a big issue for you, and obviously you're experiencing a great deal of inner conflict. I want to assist you to understand the cause of the

conflict. Let's do some regression work. Center yourself."
(pause) "All right, I now want to go back to the cause of
your conflict with men; back to the cause of fearing a loss
of freedom, and fearing sex, responsibilities and compromise. On the count of three, you'll speak up and tell
me what you perceive. One, two, three."

Trainee: "I'm in a small cabin, cooking, I think. Yes, I'm
cooking." (tired, emotionless voice)

Dick: "You have the power and ability to look around.
Describe the cabin to me. Tell me if there is anyone else
there with you."

Trainee: "My man is at the table. The room is very
small. There are a couple of windows that are frosted
over; it's winter ... it's very cold, even inside. I'm wrapped
in something but I'm still shivering."

Dick: "What is the current year?"

Trainee: "Don't know ... 1842 or maybe '43 or '44. I've
lost track. It doesn't matter."

Dick: "Will you please tell me about your life?"

Trainee: "Not much to tell. Harold hunts and I grow a
few things. We survive. That's all you can hope to do."

Dick: "How old are you?"

Trainee: "Ahhh, I guess 41."

Dick: "How long have you lived here in this cabin?"

Trainee: "Oh, 15 years ... no, that's not right. Closer to
18, I guess. But when I was young, I lived in New York
City and it was wonderful. Life was gay and happy. My
mistake in life was going West."

Dick: "Did you meet Harold in the West?"

Trainee: "Yes, after my family died. He took me in and
fed me in exchange for favors."

Dick: "What do you mean, 'favors'?"

Trainee: "You know ... favors. He had his way with me."

Dick: "Tell me about Harold. Describe him to me."

Trainee: "Not much to tell. He's a big man and he hunts.

I cook, and we survive."

Dick: "Is Harold big and also fat?"

Trainee: "Oh, yes. Very, very fat."

Dick: "All right, Diana. On the count of three, you'll be back in the present time, but you'll remember everything you just experienced. One, two, three." (awakening) "I hope you can see that your subconscious and conscious minds are out of alignment. Subconsciously, you fear that if you establish a relationship with a man, you will once again begin to experience the drudgery and depression that must have accompanied the incarnation with Harold. The fear from the past life is acting as a block to love in this life. You must now let go of the fear. Maybe just knowing the cause will resolve the conflict. If it doesn't, you may have to confront the fear by acting anyway. And you can begin immediately to deprogram yourself in daily hypnosis or meditation. Tell yourself, 'I now know the cause of my conflict with men and I choose to let go of it. I know the past cannot affect the present unless I allow it, and I now free myself to create the space in my life for the right relationship with a man … a man with whom I can experience a happy, fulfilling relationship of love and growth.'"

Never do anything that you'll have to punish yourself for.

19.

Trainee: "You say that the Master of Life will maintain a perspective of involved detachment with his primary relationship?"

Dick: "With his life."

Trainee: "Well, that just sounds kind of cold to me. Enjoy all the warm times and if she gets nasty just remain stoic like a wooden Indian. She'd think I didn't care!"

Dick: "Does your lady know you care by your exhibition of fear? Any reaction other than a calm, quiet, or warm approach would be fear. Detached doesn't mean cold or dead. It means that you love someone enough to allow them to be what they need to be regardless of how nasty they may become. It is kindness, compassion and open-hand love."

Trainee: "Oh, bullshit! If she yells at me and I yell back, we both know that we care enough to react to each other."

Dick: "That's exactly why your relationships don't work, Bob. That's why, after all these years, you are still yelling. That's resistance and resistance is fear."

Trainee: "I just can't buy it."

Dick: "Then don't buy it, Bob. Nobody cares if you buy it or not. You think love is supposed to be fear, just like 99 percent of the world. Fine. How many other people in this room can see how Bob is stuck in this area?"

Trainees: (nearly every hand goes up)

Trainee: "Let's look at it another way. What if I really flirted with another woman and my wife saw me? If she just acted calm about it, I'd think she didn't care."

Dick: "Her love for you is then measured by how fearfully she responds to your flirting with another woman? Let's assume she yells. What is that really all about? Maybe she wants control of you and figures she doesn't have it. Maybe she just wants you to be exactly what she wants you to be, and she is afraid it isn't happening. Maybe she is

81

fearful that attention shown toward another woman diminishes some attention she'll receive from you. Maybe's ... regardless of the reason, yelling is fear. Involved detachment means that you love and trust the other person so much that you support them in whatever they need to do. They are perfect from your perspective, so where do you get the right to yell in the first place?"

Trainee: "You are impossible to talk to ... you twist my words all around."

Dick: "Bob, you twist your life all around and make it difficult when it doesn't need to be that way. How is your marital relationship? BE STRAIGHT!"

Trainee: "Well, it could be a lot better, just like everyone else's. We do yell a lot, but these weird ideas of yours wouldn't do anything to improve it."

Dick: "Argue for your limitations and they become your reality."

Trainee: "All right. Let's assume I really want to react calmly to her, but in so doing, I'm repressing my real feelings. I outwardly respond calmly, but inwardly I'm boiling. That wouldn't work either."

Dick: "No, it wouldn't. These things aren't easy and instantaneous, Bob. They can be, but for most people, growth comes with awareness. As you become aware of your True Self and the realities of life, you begin to stop resisting your life. In time, you come to participate when it's fun to participate and simply observe the rest of the time."

Trainee: "The Buddha bit, huh? I guess that might be all right."

Trainee: "I admit that I'm really bothered by the fact that my ex-wife yells if I'm even the slightest bit late bringing the kids back after my weekend with them. I dwell on it for days."

Dick: "You take it personally and really get upset, right?"

Trainee: "Damned right. I can't help it."

Dick: "You're the only one who **can** help it. Does she have any other ex-husbands or are you the only one?"

Trainee: "Just me."

Dick: "What if she had another ex-husband and they also had children. Do you think she'd yell at him if he brought the kids back late?"

Trainee: "You could count on it."

Dick: "Well, then, that is what your ex-wife does. The way she reacts to you, she would react to anyone who was in your position. There is nothing personal in it, as you've just pointed out. She yells at ex-husbands who bring their children back late. So what? It's her right to yell, and it's your right not to get upset."

Trainee: "Wow, I never thought of it that way. All that upset for nothing. I can't wait for her to yell next time."

"*R*age, hate, passionate love, these are all created within ourselves, and we are truly weak if we cannot control them."
C. W. Nichol
"Moving Zen—Karate As A Way To Gentleness"

21.

Trainee: "What would you say is the most important consideration in programming success in any area of your life?"

Dick: "Be absolutely clear about your intent. Exactly what you want and to what extent you are willing to go to achieve it. Remember that the size of your vision is more important than the amount of your programming."

*Softness triumphs over
    hardness,
    feebleness over
    strength.*

*What is more malleable
    is always superior
    to that
    which is immovable.*

*This is the principle
    of controlling things
    by going along
    with them,
    of mastery
    through adaptation.*

Lao-Tzu

Trainee: "You say our viewpoint is a result of all previous subconscious programming and that includes the five physical senses?"

Dick: "Sure. Sight, sound, taste, touch and smell; and these only have meaning if you had previous experiences which relate to them."

Trainee: "Well, why ..." (struggling to hold back her emotions) "Why do I become nauseated every time I smell the smoke from a woodburning fire? We have actually had to move from a neighborhood where there were a lot of fireplaces because of the physical effects I experienced during the cold months."

Dick: "Your nausea is probably a physiological reaction to repressed emotions. All feelings and emotions come from some definite event, even if the event cannot be clearly defined or located in time. We'll be doing many sessions in here to discover such things, but let's find out what the cause is for you right now. Use your technique and go up to your center." (pause) "All right, on the count of three, very strong impressions will begin to come in. You will see or sense or know what is transpiring. These impressions will relate to your present aversion to the smell of woodsmoke. One, two, three. Trust what is coming in."

Trainee: "I perceive a young boy riding a horse. It's grassy country and he seems to be having fun."

Dick: "Move forward in time until something important happens."

Trainee: "There is smoke over there. He's ... I'm riding toward it. It's a house made out of logs . . or it was a house—it's all burned down now, just smoke rising in the air. I'm riding quickly up to the remains; I'm scared. Oh, God ... Oh, my God! My mommy and daddy are in there!

That's **MY** house!" (The trainee begins to gag and choke.) "Oh, my God! I can't ... I can't ..."

Dick: "Yes, you can. I want you to fully understand this. Don't talk any more, just experience." (two or three minutes pass in silence) "Do you fully understand what transpired here?"

Trainee: (nodding sadly) "Yes."

Dick: "Okay. You will return to full consciousness and be with me. At the count of three, you will awaken, feeling calm and relaxed. One, two, three."

Trainee: "Oh, wow! That was awful! The little boy ran into the burning embers of what was left of the house. The smell from the smoke billowing around him was awful. He stumbled over the remains of his mother and fell into the smoldering embers. He was badly burned. He was only about six or seven years old. He didn't get up again ... I got that he died there, very, very slowly. I have no idea where this happened, whether it was early America, Europe or what. There was a painted, decorated pole that I saw that looked more Scandinavian than anything else."

Dick: "A magnitude 1 experience like this could easily carry the effect forward into successive lifetimes. It may very well be that in understanding the cause, you can release the effect."

Trainee: "I can't wait to smell a fireplace!"

Note: The trainee later wrote and told us that her aversion to the smell of burning wood was no longer a problem, but qualified it by explaining that she still had no desire for a fireplace.

23

Trainee: "I get confused trying to keep up with everything that is going on in here. We jump from processes to sharings to talks and I can't keep it all straight in my head."

Dick: "You're not supposed to be keeping it straight, Adam. You're attempting to understand and that doesn't work. Just experience what you experience. Accept the insights as they relate to you."

Trainee: "But I've got to sort out what to believe and what not to believe."

Dick: "Adam! **Get that I don't want you to believe a damned thing!** I've made that abundantly clear several times, but evidently, you were too busy trying to figure out what to believe to hear me. A belief is your opinion. It's something you don't know. You may think you know. You might even be willing to stake your life on the fact that you know. But you don't know. A belief is a prejudice with no supporting experience. So don't believe ... **EXPERIENCE!** Wisdom grows out of experience."

Trainee: "Well, this is a weird seminar."

Dick: "And that's what is, Adam."

Trainee: "Well, I really didn't like all the people crying in that last process."

Dick: "Now we're getting down to what's going on with you, aren't we? What bothered you about the session, Adam?"

Trainee: "There was absolutely no justification or need for it."

Dick: "You're judging from your viewpoint, Adam. It's **a faulty assumption** to presume that since you didn't get anything out of it, neither did anyone else." (turns toward group) "All right, in the last 'victim/bad guy' session, how many of you feel a release in experiencing that there are no victims and no one to blame?" (three-fourths of the hands are raised)

Trainee: "Well, I think it's weird that they got off on that!"

Dick: "How does this reflect in your life, Adam? How else do you judge from your viewpoint in ways that cause conflict?"

Trainee: "I don't know what you're talking about."

Dick: "Yes, you do."

Trainee: "You f---king FASCIST! I DON'T BELIEVE THIS!"

Dick: "Adam, who isn't the way you want them to be? What isn't the way you want it to be?"

Trainee: "Well, there is plenty of room for improvement in a lot of people. What's that got to do with it?"

Dick: "I want to hear precisely about who needs to improve."

Trainee: "My wife and her stupid family. Sally's priorities are certainly screwed up and her family is one step removed from cavemen. When my wife tolerates the way they act, she encourages that behavior."

Dick: "And that's what you believe?"

Trainee: "That's what is, as you would say."

Dick: "And you fight with your wife about this?"

Trainee: "Yes! And I'm sick of it. She gives me a constant knot in my stomach."

Dick: "She gives you the knot? Adam, you give yourself the knot in your stomach. Again, as Buddha said, 'It is your resistance to what is that causes your suffering.' What is, is Sally supports her family. It is **your** resistance to what is that is causing the knot in your stomach. Can't you see that?"

Trainee: "She's my wife! She should support me before her family."

Dick: "And if you could have her do anything you wanted her to do, what would that be?"

Trainee: "Tell them all to get lost!"

Dick: "Oh, just give them up? And what would that prove to you, Adam?"

Trainee: "That she loves me!"

Dick: "She can't love her family and you too? Why are you so insecure, Adam?"

Trainee: "**I'm not insecure!** You're the problem here. I've never seen anyone who can turn things around like you can. You're actually trying to make **me** out to be the bad guy."

Dick: "WHY ARE YOU SO INSECURE, ADAM?"

Trainee: "YOU F--CKING ..."

Dick: "WHY ARE YOU SO INSECURE, ADAM?"

Trainee: "Two women have left me. They said they loved me, then one day they just walked out of my life. If Sally really loves me, she'll put me before her family."

Dick: "Sally has more than enough love for both you and her family but if you force her to make a choice, she may just choose those who aren't asking her to choose."

Trainee: "That's it. Nobody really loves anybody!"

Dick: "Oh, come on, Adam. Is that the lesson? GET OFF IT!"

Trainee: (He begins to cry and refuses to continue the dialogue.)

Dick: "I think Adam is getting it, and I'm sure the rest of you can see why he is experiencing distress. It's easy to see it in others, but we avoid this awareness in ourselves. The questions to be asking yourself right now are those regarding your own **faulty assumptions.**"

24

Trainee: "I can see how Adam's resistance and assumptions are messing up his life, but in my case, the people I work with are literally giving me an ulcer. I'm not asking anything of them but for them to leave me alone. I don't think I'm resisting the woman who is behind the hatefulness because I really don't care if she lives or dies."

Dick: "You are talking cause and effect, Gloria. If **they** are giving you the ulcer, you have to be reacting to them."

Trainee: "But the old bitch who is assistant supervisor has turned everyone against me. I'm not making that up."

Dick: "I'm not saying you are. When people hate, they always look for allies. The less justified the grievance, the more pressing the desire for allies. The more someone wrongs someone they hate, the more fuel they add to their hatred. And that is the way humans work. The one who hates has to silence her guilty conscience and she does this by convincing herself and others that you really de- serve punishment. She cannot feel indifference or pity for someone wronged; she must hate and persecute or else leave the door open to self-contempt. Hatred can give meaning to an empty life. So get that your adversary is to be pitied. You can send her love and you might directly confront her in a very positive way. Above all, you can realize that it is your reaction to her that is causing your stomach problems. And since you are doing it to yourself, it is you who must resolve the problem by allowing the negativity to flow through you without affecting you."

Trainee: "Because I can't change other people?"

Dick: "Right, it is only within your power to change how you react to them. Your assistant supervisor is a hateful bitch, and that's what is. Now you have two choices . . . you can stay or quit and find another job."

Trainee: "Oh, I don't want to quit, I'm getting fantastic experience."

Dick: "Okay, now you've got two more choices. You can allow yourself to be upset by what is, resulting in an ulcer, or you can begin to consciously detach and allow the negativity to flow through you without affecting you."

Trainee: "You make it sound so simple."

Dick: "It is simple, but that doesn't mean easy."

Trainee: "All right, I want to develop detached mind. And I already know you're going to tell me that my expectations are in conflict with what is. So I look at the logic and remind myself that I have expectations of approval or control every time I start to become upset. Plus, I can directly confront her and I suppose I can use some stress reduction techniques in self-hypnosis. Anything else?"

Dick: "See? You didn't need me."

*N*atural man analyzes:
    taking all things
    and concepts apart
    to see
    how they tick.

*T*he Master of Life synthesizes:
    finding unity in diversity,
    wholeness in separateness,
    and seeing the oneness
    at the heart of all things.

25.

Trainee: "My wife always yells at me that I think of myself first."

Dick: "That's because she wants you to think of her first; you're not being the way she wants you to be. Of course, she is right in that everyone puts their own self-interest first. Your mistake would be to take it personally. If you let her anger upset you, be aware that you are recognizing something in her that exists within yourself. She is a 'mirror' for you, even though you don't consciously realize it. If her anger really bothers you, Jim, be aware that there is plenty of repressed anger in you."

*A man who has
attained mastery
of an art
reveals it
in his
every action.*

Samurai maxim

Dick: "As a simple little self-esteem process, get used to asking yourself a question before you act. **'Am I gaining power or losing power by acting this way?'** Don't give away your power. You give away your self-esteem, thus you program yourself the wrong way. A grade school teacher recently made the news because she was concerned about maintaining her students' self-esteem. She noticed that when the students were ready to bring their papers to her desk, they raised their hands and asked, 'Miss Williams, may I bring my paper to your desk now?', resulting in a loss of their personal power. Instead, she asked them to raise their hand and state, 'Miss Williams, I am bringing my paper to your desk now.' Thus, the students maintained their power and increased their sense of self-esteem."

> *To win one hundred*
> *victories*
> *in one hundred*
> *battles*
> *is not the*
> *highest skill.*
>
> *To subdue the enemy*
> *without fighting*
> *is the*
> *highest skill.*
>
> *Sun-Tzu*

Trainee: "I've listened to everything you've said about guilt, but I still feel guilty. I fell in love with another man and I ended up divorcing my husband because of it and that separated my children from their real father."

Dick: "Exactly what do you feel guilty about, Charlene?"

Trainee: "I feel guilty about the whole situation."

Dick: "No! The whole situation is a concept. You can't feel guilty about a concept. EXACTLY what do you feel guilty about, Charlene?"

Trainee: "I caused my children to be separated from their father."

Dick: "You did that all by yourself? That's interesting. In all my days of working with people who have relationship problems, I've never seen a totally one-sided marital situation."

Trainee: "Well, my husband didn't show me the least bit of affection for years prior to the affair."

Dick: "I'm not interested in your seemingly reasonable justifications. There are no victims in life. When you realize that, you can stop seeking causes which may not relate at all to the situation. Everyone is totally responsible for what happens to them. Can you get that, Charlene?"

Trainee: "Well, yes, I accept karma. I accept that."

Dick: "Then your husband experienced what he needed to experience. Right? How can it be that your children aren't also responsible for what happens to them?"

Trainee: "All right. But why do I feel guilty?"

Dick: "Why do **you** suppose you feel guilty, Charlene?"

Trainee: (shrugging) "I don't know."

Dick: "Maybe when all this sinks in, you won't feel guilty. I don't think you have gotten it yet. WHAT IS, IS. The facts are that you fell in love with someone else and got a divorce. That's over and done, and yet as long as you continue to resist what happened, you're going to be imprisoned within it. As Buddha taught, our suffering results from the way we resist our lives. You have a choice to feel guilty or not to feel guilty. Either way, the situations in your life remain outwardly the same. One way you suffer; the other way you don't. Simple. Can you make this all right with yourself, Charlene?"

Trainee: "I guess I've been punishing myself, huh?"

Dick: (long, hard look at Charlene)

Trainee: "I know you're right. It isn't doing me any good. If I want to stop, all I have to do is ... ah ... oh, to HELL with that guilt!"

Trainees: (spontaneous applause)

*We are not punished
for our sins,
but by them.*

Buddhist saying

28.

Trainee: "I really don't like what you just communicated to Charlene. It sounds to me like you are providing people with the ultimate cop-out. They don't have to be responsible for what they do. She should feel damn guilty for what she did."

Dick: "It couldn't be that a woman left you at one time for another man, could it, George?"

Trainee: "That's right, but that doesn't have anything to do with it."

Dick: "It has everything to do with it. Why did your wife leave you for another man, George?"

Trainee: "I'm not standing up here to talk about that. I want to talk about the irresponsibility of your philosophy."

Dick: "That's exactly what we are talking about, George, so you just go along with me and prove how wrong I am. **Why did your wife leave you for another man, George?**"

Trainee: "She said she wanted to enjoy life and off she went. She liked parties and things like that and I didn't, so what?"

Dick: "So that is all bullshit! That is George looking for life to be reasonable from his limited perspective. You look at everything from that perspective and the result is that your life is filled with stress, tension and anxiety. If you want your life to start working, stop looking for it to be fair or reasonable from an earthbound perspective. I want you to use your technique and center yourself, George. All right, I am now going to count from one to three, and on the count of three, you will have moved back in time to the cause of your wife leaving you. The cause. No cop-outs ... be straight, George. We're going to go back in time just as far as it takes to look at the primary cause. One, two, three. Speak up and tell me what is happening at this time."

Trainee: "I see ... well, I feel and see—it's like a faint fantasy—a woman working in a factory. It's really an ugly environment. She is tired and there are many other women there, too. It is an awful place to work."

Dick: "All right, on the count of three, new impressions will come in that will assist us in understanding what is going on. One, two, three."

Trainee: "I see her now with three children. The children are dressed as badly as she is and they all live in a little bitty room. They are eating dinner and they have hardly anything at all."

Dick: "Where is her husband?"

Trainee: "I don't know!"

Dick: "Where is her husband?"

Trainee: "He left her. I think ... I think I was her husband. Oh, Lord, I wouldn't have done that!"

Dick: "Oh, really? **Did** you do that? **Did you leave your wife and three children? FACE IT!"**

Trainee: "Yes, I did!" (crying)

Dick: "On the count of three, you will be wide awake, fully alert and back in the room. One, two, three."

Trainee: "I left her last time and she did it to me this time. She lived a drab miserable life, and so this time around, she wanted to enjoy herself."

Dick: "That is still looking for things to be reasonable, tied up in a neat little package, George. There may have been other lives in between, and there were causes and effects that may go way back, prior to what you just experienced. The cause isn't important once you get that **you and you alone** are responsible for everything that happens to you!"

Trainee: "I'm sorry I challenged you."

Dick: "Don't be sorry. That gives away your power. Let's go back to the original situation for a moment. You felt Charlene should feel guilty. You wanted to see punishment bestowed on Charlene. Right? Well, I want everyone in this room to get that you're the one who punishes you. No one else punishes you. No one else has to. We are all so good at doing it to ourselves that we don't need anyone else to do it. It may very well be that Charlene has simply perpetrated her karma with her husband and will go through future balance with him. I'm not excusing Charlene or providing anyone with a cop-out. Charlene can forgive herself when she finally learns about human relationships. At that time, she'll have the intuitive wisdom and she'll no longer experience relationship problems. She can explore other learning."

Trainee: "You're speaking from a perspective of many lifetimes."

Dick: "Yes, and it could all be settled in this lifetime. It depends upon the current level of awareness, and the willingness to let go."

29.

Trainee: "I don't have it straight. Charlene left her husband. She could have remained in the environment of a man who didn't show her any affection. That's a great choice: damned if you do and damned if you don't."

Dick: "There is simply no way for us to understand all the karmic interaction going on for Charlene or for anyone else for that matter. Instead of attempting to do that, let's explore choice for a moment. When you come up against an opportunity or crisis in your life, you have to make a decision as to what to do. In most situations, there will be several alternative courses to take. I feel that you predetermined the crisis as a learning opportunity, but you have free will to react to it in any way you choose.

"Hopefully, you will be able to apply the intuitive knowledge from your past experiences or failures to take the directions which will lead to the learning you require of yourself.

"When you decide which direction and go forward on a particular path, you will have to take all its consequences and you may be forced to go on for a very long way before you have the opportunity to change direction. Think of it this way: you drive your car to a particular destination (goal) and come to an intersection (crisis) that branches into three different freeways. Whichever freeway you choose will be the direction you will go until you come to the next intersection. Freeway Number One will get you to your destination in the most direct way possible. Freeway Number Two may wander around a bit, but is still going in the general direction of your destination. Freeway Number Three would actually carry you in the wrong direction.

"Each freeway will have more intersections as you travel them and you will have to make a decision at each intersection as to which path you will travel. From a metaphysical perspective, Freeway Number One, the most direct path, would also be the hardest. You would be taking on the most difficult high speed road to your destination. In so doing, you hope you can handle the burden you are accepting. You hope you won't crash your car. If this should be the end result, you would actually be further than ever from your destination and would have been better off taking Freeway Number Two, where this would have been less likely to happen.

"As an analogy, let's take this understanding into a possible marital situation. You're a woman and you've been married for some time and love your husband very much, but you just found out that he is having an affair with his secretary. He loves her and is indecisive about leaving you, but he finally decides he would prefer to stay with you if you still want him. Assume you have decided upon three alternatives, three freeways from which to choose:

"Freeway #1—The Hardest: You tell him, 'Real love for another person cannot be diminished by anything they say or do. I want to remain married to you as long as you want me because I love you and that love is not dependent upon your loving me in return. I give you total freedom, expecting no more from you than what you can freely give. I don't expect you to be anything other than what you are. I love you for what you are, and I'll find joy in the time you want to spend with me.'

"Freeway #2—Moderation: You tell him, 'I love you and I want to remain married to you, but I am extremely hurt by your actions. I certainly want you to find a new secretary. It may be difficult for me not to think about this for a while, but I desire to let go of it and I want to restore my trust in you.'

"Freeway #2—Alternative: You tell him, 'I love you, I wish I were a big enough person to overlook what you have done, but I'm afraid that if we remain together right now, I will become possessive and vindictive. I don't want this to happen so I think it best that we separate for a while to decide what the best future direction might be. I would prefer all future interaction, regardless of what directions we go, to be without hostility or animosity.'

"Freeway #3—Wrong Direction: You tell him, 'Well, two people can play this game. If you want to remain with me, you are going to get a taste of your own medicine because I know plenty of men who will jump at the chance to go to bed with me. You're about to find out just how vindictive I can be. You'll pay for this little escapade for the next five years.'

"All right, let's look at the choices now. If you picked Freeway Number One, you are now on that road. If you could sincerely react to the situation in this manner, you would have a very high level of awareness in the area of personal relationships. You have made many statements that you will now have to live up to, but do you have the ability to handle this beautiful but idealistic outlook? It may be hard to ever trust him again, hard not to dwell on the entire situation, hard not to think vindictive thoughts. If you say one thing and think another, you will be building resentments and hostilities and these emotions will always come out in one form or another. When they do, it could totally destroy your marriage. If you can't handle the road, you may crash the car, thus programming more negative karma that will need to be balanced in the future. If this should happen, you would have been better off choosing Freeway Number Two, which would have been easier to handle and would have kept you on the proper, though slower, pathway to your destination."

30.

Trainee: "Where does predestination fit into all of this?"

Dick: "You may have predetermined some of the crisis situations in your life but you certainly didn't predestine your reactions to them. You always have free will."

Trainee: "Then how can a psychic read what is going to happen in the future?"

Dick: "The psychic can only read potentials. Potentials that already exist and are there in your mind. If you've been fighting with your husband for three years and it gets worse every year, the potential for separation is increasing. Still, it is a potential, not a predestined event."

Trainee: "An astrologer told a friend of mine in August that she'd be divorced the following May and it happened."

Dick: "Anyone who is stupid enough to go to a psychic or astrologer and let them provide you with that sort of programming must need that learning, yet a little wisdom could certain save considerable misery. If someone you respect enough to pay a good deal of money for their advice tells you that a divorce is predestined, how are you going to put that out of your mind? No one could. You begin to live with that in mind and thus begin to create the final programming for the divorce. The potential for the divorce may have been there. The astrology chart may have indicated a weakness in the relationship area in May, but there is always more than one way to read any aspect. It was never predestined, but because she thought it was, guess what? It was.

"There is a glacier up north that is moving south at the rate of six inches a year. It's been doing so for thousands of years. Its potential to move south another six inches this year is pretty strong but it is **not** predestined. An inverse ratio of snowfall to snow melt could retard or even reverse the process."

31.

Trainee: "I'd like to know how you perceive God."

Dick: "You're God, I'm God ... we are all God. To be symbolic for a moment, let's assume that once there was a great energy gestalt we'll call God. And God allowed a great deal of his energy to break off into separate pieces as a form of procreation and expansion of the original energy.

"I like the analogy of a single cell in your body. Assume for a moment that you are just one of the billions of cells in your body. If our cloning abilities were as developed in humans as they are in reptiles, that cell would be all that would be necessary to clone a duplicate of you. The cell has the potential of the original, containing a complete blueprint for the entire body. The cell is a part of Elaine's body that I see standing here before me, yet the cell is also Elaine. You part of the great body of God, and you are also God.

"Jesus said this himself when he responded to those

speaking of the miracles he had performed, saying, 'These things ye too shall do and more.' We have the power to accomplish what men call miracles. Understanding that **we are God** can result in an immediate transformation of the way we experience life."

32.

Dick: "We've talked a great deal about how the mind works like a computer, and since we are mind, that makes us machines ... robots. We all have computer buttons; when they get pushed, you become a robot and demonstrate your automatic responses. You see, a robot has no choice in the way it acts. It has wiring and circuits constructed so that, when a button is pushed, it reacts according to its programming. And in so many areas of your life you're a robot; that's a major reason your life doesn't work as well as it could.

"You can't change what you don't recognize, so it is time to recognize your automatic responses and learn to override them. It's time to stop going on 'tilt' when someone or something pushes one of your buttons. 'Tilt' is when you stop functioning rationally.

"All right. Go up to your center." (altered-state induction given) "Let's explore a few of your buttons. What causes you to react? As I ask you some questions, be straight with yourself and trust the very first thought that comes into your mind. What causes you to become angry quickly?" (pause) "What embarrasses you?" (pause) "What really irritates you about your mate?" (pause) "What really bothers you in your career?" (pause) "What causes you to become fearful?" (pause) "What pushes your sexual buttons off and on?" (pause) "Does what other people think control you in any particular area?" (pause) "What is it that you fear them thinking or knowing?" (pause) "How does what other people think manipulate you?" (pause)

"Can you get that you've been programmed? Brainwashed from birth to worry about what other people think? You grew up worrying about what others think. Your parents worried about what other people thought. But what others think may not be in your best interest. What **YOU** think is most important. There is really no such thing as right and wrong, ethical and unethical, moral and immoral. A society, which is a group of people, agrees upon what terminology to use regarding a particular action; maybe they agree to call it moral or immoral. That doesn't make it either moral or immoral, it only makes it what that group labels moral or immoral. Their naming it one thing or another cannot change what it is. In some countries, eating cattle is immoral. In other countries, the word 'rape' is not a part of the language—not even a concept, for the men assume the right to take women by force whenever they desire to do so. In some areas of the world, open sexuality is considered moral and beautiful.

"When living in a society, we must be willing to accept the consequences of our actions regarding the laws of the society, yet most of the conflicts with the opinions of others are not legal issues. It may be ill-advised for you to allow the opinions of others to push your reaction buttons and cause you to repress what you really are. Think about how this relates to your life." (pause)

"Okay, we've explored just a few of your buttons. When they get pushed, you react quickly, and this will rarely be in your best interests. You know this. You are reacting to the button, to the old programming, not to what is. You need to become consciously aware of all your buttons, and when you awaken, we're going to explore a technique to hold back in your immediate inclination to react."

33

Dick: "In regard to your buttons: I'm not saying to repress what you are, I am simply saying that if you hold back in your initial inclination to react immediately to anger, fear, or adoration, your life will work better. The idea is to catch yourself long enough to think about your reaction.

"A martial arts student is taught to keep his 'mind like calm water,' because if he allows himself to become angry or fearful, he greatly reduces his potential to win in an encounter. To keep your mind like calm water accurately reflects everything within striking range.

"Instead of reacting to extreme emotions, go into a calm inner space where you calculate the best response to get what you want. The goal is to win the game, not to be right. But as a robot, your subconscious computer has one primary goal: **survival.** It achieves that goal by comparing the present to the past. This means, in essence, that your subconscious computer says it is all right for you to live your life just as you do.

"It has survived so far and it knows that it did it by being right. According to computer logic, it **has** to be right. Of course, you know consciously that you aren't always right ... but your subconscious doesn't. So, it responds to programming and you get to be right, but you lose the game. When you are challenged, you become indignant. Your button is pushed and you react quickly. And, as you probably know from experience, this is rarely in your best interest.

"You are reacting to the button, **not** to what is. So you need to be consciously aware of your programming instead of subconsciously reacting to it. It is part of the **Bushido** code that 'the strong are patient.' Patience in this case means to hold back in your immediate inclination to respond to the extreme emotions of anger, fear, and adoration."

Trainee: "I don't understand why you include adoration as one of the three extreme emotions."

Dick: "Okay, let's say you are married, Louise, but you meet someone and your infatuation is so intense that you respond to the offer to go to bed with him. You've broken an agreement, so at the very least, you're going to have sacrificed self-esteem, which is negative programming. Or maybe your husband finds out about it and the result is a weakened marriage. Or, in today's society, the result could be AIDS or some other sexual disease."

Trainee: "But how can you overcome a lifetime of conditioning to obtain the kind of control you're talking about?"

Dick: "It would have to begin with the desire, wouldn't it? You would have to realize that you'll be better served by changing the way you react to others. Next, a technique such as 'mudra' can be of great supportive value.

"Touch your index finger and thumb together to form the mudra position. This is a post-programming technique which can be fully conditioned in about three weeks if you include it every day as part of your self-hypnosis or meditation session. In an altered state, tell yourself, 'whenever I purposely connect my index finger and thumb, I will immediately become calm and peaceful. The mudra finger position is a conditioned response key to my subconscious mind and when I use it, I will immediately experience an internal balance and harmony that will allow me to override my extreme emotions, giving me time to think calmly about my reactions. And every time I give myself this suggestion, every time I use the mudra finger positioning, it will become more powerful.'"

34

Trainee: "My wife wanted me to attend this training because we aren't getting along at all well. Now I'm getting that it was an attempt to manipulate me into thinking the same way she does."

Dick: "And..."

Trainee: "Obviously, I'm going to be able to communicate better with her because now I'll understand where she is coming from. But it's not a big deal."

Dick: "Any marriage counselor will tell you that the primary problem they see in dealing with troubled couples is lack of communication. One partner doesn't know how the other really feels because there has been no direct communication on the subject. Both assume they know and have thus established distorted concepts based on their own viewpoints, which are not accurate.

"We all need positive feedback from those closest to us. Sadly enough, it is our intimate relationships that are most often ignored. Do you tell your wife you love her?"

Trainee: "Of course—I married her, didn't I?"

Dick: "Never count on the fact that the other person knows anything you haven't directly communicated. Your wife may not show her emotional needs but would give anything to hear those three words from you. The fact that she doesn't hear them could result in doubting thoughts about the relationship, which creates negative computer programming. Do you love her, Murphy?"

Trainee: "Of course I do. I wish we got along better, but I sure love her."

Dick: "Great! Then express your real feelings. Stop blocking your True Self and say what you feel, not just to your wife, but to all who are close to you. 'I love you.' 'You're fantastic.' 'I've been thinking about you.' Never assume that the other person knows how you feel."

35.

Trainee: "I was married for eight years to the perfect man and we had the perfect kids and the perfect house. Everybody in town envied us. Then, out of the clear blue, he just divorced me. That was two years ago and I still haven't gotten over it."

Dick: "Well, your choices are clear, aren't they, Anne? You can get over it or not get over it. Obviously, no one else cares what you do. One way you suffer, the other way you don't."

Trainee: "Oh, that is really a lot of help!"

Dick: "I don't have any help for you, Anne. Only you can help yourself. What could I do?"

Trainee: "Give me some advice."

Dick: "Okay, the same advice I give to the world: **Accept that what is, is!**"

Trainee: "Since this whole seminar started, I have liked you and I have hated you. Right now, you're not at the top of my list, you know."

Dick: "Anne, at the beginning of this training, I told you that would be the case, remember? I also told you that you'd be depressed, angry, bored and that you'd probably laugh and cry. Right now, I'm not being the way you want me to be, just the way your husband wasn't the way you wanted him to be."

Trainee: "He was almost perfect."

Dick: (just stares at her)

Trainee: "Well, he certainly was in most ways. He was handsome and he was an excellent provider and really good with the kids. It was really his wanting me to be other than what I am."

Dick: "How was that?"

Trainee: "Well, he ... he always wanted sex. You know. Men sometimes get carried away that way. I didn't share his enthusiasm for that portion of our relationship."

Dick: "Why is it that I see you as wanting your perfect husband to have a more perfect sex drive? How is it that you've turned that part around, Anne?"

Trainee: "Well, so what? He made up for it all right. He found a little cutie and gave up everything for her."

Dick: "That's what you got out of it, Anne. That may not be the way he views it at all. Regardless, something that happened in the past is blocking your experiencing the present, the now. Your husband divorced you, that's what is. You can let go of it and get on with your life or you can continue to chew on it and thus program your computer for a more negative reality in the future."

Trainee: "What do you think about me really experiencing my resentments and hostility, like you told that man over there? Then I could start with hypnosis programming."

Dick: "What do you think about that?"

Trainee: "I'm going to do it."

> "... many attacks are initiated
> by the victim. If a person
> is feeling bad about himself and
> unconsciously desires to be hurt,
> he will draw his attacker to
> himself. Or instead, he may just
> have a car accident or some other
> injury. So it is important
> to know yourself thoroughly."
>   Dr. Terry Chitwood
>   "How To Defend Yourself
>   Without Even Trying"

Trainee: "I don't see why you bother exploring some of the dumb aspects of people's belief systems. We're not here for that. We want to learn new things."

Dick: "The most famous Zen story of all is about Nan-in, a Japanese master. It seems that a university professor visited him to inquire about Zen. Nan-in asked his visitor if he'd like tea and the professor accepted. Nan-in served the tea, pouring his visitor's cup full ... and kept pouring. The professor watched the overflow until he could no longer restrain himself. 'It is full to overflowing. No more will go in!'

"Nan-in replied, 'Like this cup, you are full of your own opinions and speculations. How can I show you Zen unless you first empty your cup?'

"This training is more about deprogramming than it is about new knowledge. All your life you've been brain-washed by parents, peers and society with misconceptions, invalid views, convictions, moralities and notions that are restricting your life. Until you begin to question these traps, they'll block you. Once you realize that there is nobody out there who will save your ass or care about what you think, you can let go of the silly assumptions and get on with living, realizing that the only meaning in your life is what you bring to it."

Trainee: "These ideas make me feel kind of empty."

Dick: "New ideas are seldom immediately comfortable. Yet would you rather base your life upon pretense or upon knowledge?"

Trainee: "Knowledge. But where does it leave us?"

Dick: "Exactly where we have always been, and with clearer vision. I'm talking about a way of liberation; let your life become a beautiful spiritual pilgrimage, an exploration into creativity and joy."

Trainee: "As long as we're talking about parents, I'd like to share that I'm 34 years old but my father still controls me. My husband hates it but I don't seem able to help myself. I'm still my daddy's little girl."

Dick: "As you said that, do you realize that your body language became that of a little girl, Celia? You even did a slight curtsy. What do you get out of being his little girl?"

Trainee: "I keep hoping to get his approval, I guess, but I never do. He wanted a boy and since he didn't have one, I've been his pal. I've gone fishing and hunting with him, but he's never said he loved me. Not once. He never told my mother he loved her, either. He is very opinionated and I try to be what he wants me to be. I know it is silly but that doesn't change what I feel."

Dick: "Obviously, Celia, you haven't accepted what your father is. He is a man who doesn't give you his approval. So what? That's what is. You can sit around for the rest of your life waiting for approval that won't ever happen or you can live not waiting for approval. One way you experience anxiety. The other way you don't."

Trainee: "Well, maybe someday before he dies, he'll say he loves me. I know he loves us, down inside."

Dick: "What if he doesn't?"

Trainee: "That would be awful. But I know he does. He really does love me."

Dick: "But that isn't enough, huh? He has to express it in the way you want it expressed before it is acceptable? Let's find out about this. Close your eyes and go up to your center, Celia. On the count of three, you'll be there. One, two, three. All right, now trust the first impression that comes in, just as you've been trained to do. Let's go back to the cause of this need for your father's approval, back to the most important single event that resulted in the present day manifestations. On the count of three, you will move back in time. One, two, three. Speak up and tell me what is happening."

Trainee: "It's my sixth birthday and my daddy is coming in the front door with some of his friends. I rush up to him and grab his leg. I'm telling him I love him. **I love you, daddy!** But he just pushes me away. He doesn't say anything, just pushes me away and goes into the other room with his friends. He shouldn't push me away like that! It's my birthday! **It's my birthday!**" (she begins to cry)

Dick: (after bringing her back) "Celia, you've lived the last 28 years wanting things to be different than what they were on your sixth birthday. You've been trying to collect your present all this time and daddy doesn't have a present for you. Daddy doesn't say, 'I love you.' He fed you and clothed you and did what he did, and that's it. That's what daddy does."

Trainee: "But that's not enough!" (still crying)

Dick: "Too bad. That's all there is. Twenty-eight years of hoping and waiting and this is how it all turned out. This is how it will always turn out. Now what?"

Trainee: "Well, that just makes me furious. I mean, really furious. I'd like to punch him! I feel so much resentment."

Dick: "Great. Go ahead and feel the resentment. Feel how much it hurts, how miserable it is. Really shitty, isn't it. **Feel it, Celia. Feel it. Experience it.**"

Trainee: (cries and clenches her fists for several minutes)

Dick: "Feel better?"

Trainee: "Yes, I really do. I really feel better."

Dick: "Now that this is out of the way, maybe you can see a little more clearly. Where do you get off wanting your father to be what you want him to be? People don't go around being what others want them to be. The only way they could do that would be to constantly repress their True Selves, and that would result in horrible mental,

112

physical or behavioral manifestations. Everybody is just what they are. Period. Fathers don't change to be what their daughters want them to be. Can you get that, Celia?"

Trainee: "Oh, my God. Yes. You said that before but I guess I couldn't see it. My situation was too all-important to qualify. Oh, wow. What a jerk I've been."

Dick: "Can you make it all right that your father has always been what he is? Can you forgive him, Celia?"

Trainee: "Oh, yes, I can. I really can."

38.

Trainee: "I really don't like it when you yell at us. I really hate it."

Dick: "I only yell if I feel it helps to break through someone's block. I only yell out of love. If I didn't care, I wouldn't bother."

Trainee: "Well, I don't like you for it."

Dick: "I couldn't care less whether you leave this ballroom liking me or not. I care very much that you leave here with your life working better than when we started Friday evening. As I told you in the beginning, I'll do whatever is necessary to make this training work for you. It is for you, remember. I take it every time I conduct it. I 'got it,' as they say in Zen, a long time ago. You haven't gotten it yet, Martha."

Trainee: "I don't care about that. I just care about yelling. You shouldn't yell. Everyone that yells should stop yelling."

Dick: "Let's find out what it is with you and yelling, Martha. Do you want to go exploring?"

Trainee: "Okay."

Dick: "Close your eyes and go up to your center. On the count of three, you'll be there. One, two, three. All right now, you are going to move backward in time to the point where you got stuck on yelling. I will count from one to three, and on the count of three, strong impressions will come in that relate to the source of your anxiety about yelling. One, two, three. Speak up and tell me what is coming in for you."

Trainee: "People. Lots of people. They're running. They're all dressed in medieval costumes. They're screaming in panic. I can't see myself; I don't know what … Oh, God, there are barbarians … they're killing all the people, yelling and laughing and killing. Oh, my God, I don't believe human beings can act that way—it's awful!" (she begins to cry)

Dick: (after bringing her back) "Every time you respond to someone yelling in your present life, you are actually responding to an ancient barbarian who died a long, long time ago. Can you see how that works, Martha? A mag 1 experience in a past life caused your conscious and subconscious minds to be out of alignment with regard to the subject of yelling."

Trainee: "Got it!"

*N*othing whatever
is hidden;

From of old,
all is clear
as daylight.

The Zenrin Kushu

Trainee: "I don't see how believing destroys experience."

Dick: "What have you really looked forward to in the last year, Janis?"

Trainee: "Well, my girlfriend and I really looked forward to taking a cruise from Los Angeles down to Central America and back."

Dick: "Did you have a lot of fantasies about it prior to the trip?"

Trainee: "Yes, I guess I did. Especially about meeting eligible men."

Dick: "What else did you fantasize about before taking the trip?"

Trainee: "Oh, how neat it would be in the tropical countries. Picturesque things like that, romantic days in the sun, plus all the great food on board the ship."

Dick: "How did it all work out, Janis? Be straight."

Trainee: "Truthfully?"

Dick: (just stares at her)

Trainee: "Well, there weren't any eligible men on board that I wanted anything to do with. The one guy I liked was gay. The countries weren't picturesque, they were depressing. The days in the sun were boring because there wasn't any action. I will say the food was good, but I gained eight pounds, so I could have skipped that, too."

Dick: "Janis, if you'd taken that trip without preconceived beliefs about what it was going to be like, you might have enjoyed it. Instead, your beliefs about what it would be destroyed your experience of the trip. When there were no eligible men, you were disappointed. Obviously, you were disappointed again and again. If you had experienced each portion of the trip as it occurred, experiencing your experience for what it was, not for what you expected it to be, you might have enjoyed your vacation."

40.

Trainee: "I'd like to know why my old relationship seems to block any new involvements. I divorced my husband four years ago, but I can't let go of him. I can't commit to another man. Every time I get serious about someone new, my husband is there in my mind—and not in a positive way, either. I certainly don't want to think about him, yet it just comes in."

Dick: "All right, Audrea, use your technique and go up to your center." (pause) "And now, on the count of three, you'll receive strong, vivid impressions that relate to the situation with your ex-husband. One, two, three. Trust what comes in."

Trainee: (After a moment, anxiety begins to manifest.) "He's my ex-husband, but he looks so different! I'm getting impressions of Europe, probably in the Middle Ages." (pause) "Oh, I see. I was married to him, but I fell in love with his brother, who got me pregnant. My husband was quite a bit older. He found out and brought us before a public tribunal. It was awful! They cut out our tongues and left us in the square to be ridiculed for days. Then they hung us."

Dick: "All right. On the count of three, you will awaken, feeling calm and relaxed. One, two, three. Do you see how it works, Audrea? You don't need to fear your ex-husband any more. This time around, he won't cut out your tongue and hang you. The past doesn't relate to the present. Do you see how your conscious and subconscious minds are out of alignment on this issue?"

Trainee: "You mean, on a subconscious level I fear involvement with another man because I think he'll punish me again? I guess that's pretty obvious, isn't it? But what happens now?"

Dick: "First of all, I hope you will forgive your ex-husband for everything. That is a sure way to break the karmic tie. Your present awareness will probably end the problem with the other relationships. If it doesn't, you can use some of the other techniques we'll be covering during this training."

41.

Trainee: "I'm really bothered about something you said in the lecture before. When my husband chooses to watch football instead of accepting social invitations from friends, it makes me furious! According to your philosophy, I'm wanting him to be other than what he is."

Dick: "Ideally, all relationships include compromise. However, you are resisting what your husband is, Linda. He is a man who places football games in a high priority position. It is your resistance of life that causes your problems."

Trainee: "Well, that doesn't make me feel any better about it. I still resent it. He chooses football over me!"

Dick: "Linda, what is causing your problem is that you don't want your husband to have that opinion about football. Can you get that? That is what is going on with you every time you get upset at the way he thinks."

Trainee: "Yeah ... well, when you say it that way, it sounds like I'm off the wall, doesn't it?"

Dick: (just looks at her)

Trainee: "Okay, I can see that."

Dick: "What do you really enjoy, Linda?"

Trainee: "Clothes. Shopping for clothes."

Dick: "How would you like your husband to tell you clothes aren't important? You see, he no longer wants you to have your existing opinion about clothes."

Trainee: "No way, but that's not the same."

Dick: "Isn't it?"

Trainee: "Yes, I guess it is. Oh, well. Football's over in the spring!"

42.

Trainee: "I've been listening to all these women talk about their relationship problems, but my problem is my desire to reexperience the romance that my husband and I had in the beginning."

Dick: "Romance is the first stage of a relationship, the intense sexual interest and longing for the other person. Ideally, you carry some of that into the second stage, which is commitment. Commitment is based on really knowing each other. It's when you love and care for each other even after the masks are removed. A lot of couples never make it to commitment."

Trainee: "Well, we're certainly happy and committed, but he never tells me he loves me anymore."

Dick: "Does he love you?"

Trainee: "Oh, yes, but he doesn't say it."

Dick: "Would his telling you he loves you make him love you more?"

Trainee: "No, I guess it wouldn't change what is, huh?"

Dick: "What if I were to tell you that I don't think you are loving your husband correctly? I know the kind of man your husband is and I want you to start loving him according to a plan I'll give you."

Trainee: "That would be your kind of love. I don't know if your ideas about love would be right for me."

Dick: "Do you think it would be unfair for me to ask you to love him according to my ideas?"

Trainee: "Yes. I can only love him the way I know."

Dick: "Then why are you asking your husband to love you any differently than he does? He is giving you the kind of love he knows how to give. If he were to give you a gift you picked out, wrapped and gave to yourself, would it mean nearly as much as one that he thought of, wrapped and surprised you with?"

Trainee: "No, I guess it wouldn't."

Dick: "He is giving you the gift of his love, the way he picked it, wrapped it and gives it every day."

Trainee: "Thank you."

43.

Trainee: "It took a while, but now I can really understand what you mean when you say, 'Don't believe in God, experience God.' But I was raised Catholic and I'm still stuck on heaven and hell."

Dick: "To me, heaven and hell are symbols that relate to the here and now. When you experience peace, balance and harmony, you experience heaven. When you are disharmonious and fearful, you experience hell. Heaven and hell are reflections of your consciousness."

Trainee: "I like that. I realize it isn't part of this seminar, but what do you think about the forthcoming antichrist?"

Dick: "It is my truth that the antichrist is already here and has been for a very long time. An antichrist is one who exploits in the name of Christ. Who would that be?"

Trainee: "The pope, priests and preachers!"

Dick: (smiles)

*Pride isn't always negative—
as a means to an end it can
be used profitably.*
>   *Jan Willem van de Wetering*
>   *"The Empty Mirror"*

44.

Trainee: "Both you and your ideas seem to be pretty anti-establishment. Your long hair alone says you reject the dictates of society."

Dick: "I'm anti-establishment, but I don't resist the establishment. I feel it's in my best interest to minimize my dependency upon the establishment, which is basically the government, big business and religion in the form of churches. They will always attempt to manipulate, control and enslave you mentally. They demand repression and conformity. Conformity breeds repression and kills creativity. Their message is 'Wear the right suit, cut your hair our way and act according to our rules and we'll accept you.' So you become a phony and repress what you really are, complying out of fear.

"The establishment isn't very self-actualized. It wants you to believe that all answers can be found outside yourself. Even churches want you to find your answers outside, through a preacher, priest or set of commandments. Is it any wonder the establishment is threatened by metaphysics and Eastern philosophy, which encourages you to find your answers within?"

Trainee: "But without the establishment, there would be no services ... it would be total chaos."

Dick: "Certainly, there are benefits from the establishment, and until mankind is more enlightened, there aren't going to be many alternatives. But remember, the establishment doesn't exist for you—you exist for it. It needs your body to work and make money, buy products, pay taxes and donate. It needs your body but fears your soul. If your soul is free, you may reject the dictates of the establishment."

Trainee: "I've been working at enlightenment for three years and I can't honestly say that I'm any closer today than I was when I started."

Dick: "You've been **working** very seriously at enlightenment, Randy?"

Trainee: "Very seriously!"

Dick: "Well, I can practically guarantee you that enlightenment isn't going to take place until you stop working and start playing. Replace work with relaxation and playfulness. Even with Buddha, it wasn't until he stopped seeking that he awakened, enlightened, beneath the Bodhi tree."

Trainee: "That's ridiculous!"

Dick: "Randy, your doing, in this case, is probably your undoing. You need to walk the path to enlightenment because you enjoy traveling the path, not because you desire to get where the path is going."

Trainee: "Playing is enjoyment, and there is certainly no enjoyment in attempting to attain enlightenment."

Dick: "And until there is enjoyment in the process, you won't attain it. Can you tell me why you want enlightenment, Randy?"

Trainee: "People who are enlightened are superior to those who are not."

Dick: "Randy, let's go back to square one."

*P*ut *your faith in men, not truth.*

46.

Trainee: "Why do you do these seminars and write the books you write?"

Dick: "For my own selfish satisfaction and because that's what I do."

Trainee: "I understand that because I've been through a day and a half of this seminar, but I doubt if others would understand how you mean that. They'd see that as total selfishness."

Dick: "Then that's what they would get out of it. Be aware that **I am what you think I am.** If you think I'm selfish, then that's what I am to you. If you think I'm a hero, then I'm a hero to you. I am whatever you think I am, and I've made it all right with myself for you to think whatever you want to think.

"Let's get back to your question, though. You are looking for a reason 'why.' Reasons are just rationales, excuses that attempt to justify your behavior, to attempt to justify your doing what you want to do. Reasons seldom have much to do with what is, and when you go about explaining yourself, you give away your power. I do what I do because I do it. That's why!

"Now, if the planet is in any way served by my communications, that's wonderful. I do feel that if this awareness were to become universal, to quote Alan Watts, 'The pretentious nonsense which passes for the serious business of the world would dissolve in laughter. We would see at once that the high ideals for which we are killing and regimenting each other are empty and abstract substitutes for the unheeded miracles that surround us.'—in nature and in our own existence, our own perfection."

47.

Trainee: "What do you feel is our goal of living on the earth at this time?"

Dick: "To learn to let go of all fears and to express unconditional love. It is your resistance to what is that causes our pain. Resistance is always fear. Before we can stop resisting others, we must forgive, accept, respect and love ourselves. You can only do that by getting in touch with your True Self. Once you've let go of the fears that are part of your programming, what is left is the self-actualized Master of Life. A Master of Life would express unconditional love in response to life in general."

Trainee: "You mean, to be extra nice and loving to everybody?"

Dick: "Not necessarily. Unconditional love doesn't mean 'nicey-nicey.' Unconditional love transcends blame and judgment. It is acceptance, compassion, sharing and service."

"*It's all right to have
a good time. That's one
of the most important
messages of enlightenment.*"
*Thaddeus Golas
"The Lazy Man's Guide
To Enlightenment"*

48.

Dick: "I want everyone participating to close your eyes and go up to your center." (pause) "All right, now listen closely to my words. Life is a process of preparation, and everything you have ever experienced has led up to your being the person you are now. You have experienced hard times, sadness and problems that are uniquely your own. But these problems actually have contributed satisfaction to your life, for if there were no problems to challenge you, there would be no growth. There would be no way for you to learn how to handle things and become aware of your ability to make your life work.

"Obviously, many people manifest problems. Not consciously, but subconsciously, they create challenges for themselves. So, from this moment on, the idea is to create positive challenges for yourself, instead of allowing your subconscious mind to create its own. And if you aren't ready to do that, at least alter your viewpoint. The secret to growth through problems is to look upon all problems as opportunities. The bigger the problem, the bigger the opportunity.

"And all the positive, beautiful situations in your life have also been part of creating the person you are today. All the experiences of loving and caring, the warmth and the joy, have helped to form the person who is here, sharing with me today. And all your experiences have been preparing you; you have been incubating all of your life up until this very moment. And the question is, what have you been preparing for? You have a unique background, unique abilities, unique conditioning. I want you to meditate for a few minutes upon what all of your lifetimes and all of your experiences have been preparing you for." (silence)

"You are a self-actualizing Master of Life who accepts the warmth and joy in life while detaching from the negativity by allowing it to flow through you without affecting you. You rise above the effects of fear. You open and develop psychically as you evolve spiritually. You are accountable and aware, and compassion is a way of life. You think positively and your viewpoint is to see problems only as opportunities. Each and every day, your life becomes more joyful and fulfilling. You fully realize that you are unlimited in your potential to create your own reality. And these suggestions are communicated to every level of your body and mind ... and so it is."

You are not alone.
There are others, on their way on the same track.
Travelers from nowhere to nowhere, on their way
    from nothing to nothing.
The track may be narrow and steep and boring
    and frightening but everybody walks on it.
You are not alone but linked to everything around you.
        Jan Willem van de Wetering
        "A Glimpse of Nothingness"

Participants in any Sutphen Seminar may ask for the microphone and interact with Dick Sutphen if they desire, but they are never forced or asked individually to share. The majority who attend participate in the regressions and self-exploration sessions, and observe without interacting.

Out of the context of the seminar, trainer techniques often appear cold and unfeeling to a reader. In reality, they are a form of "hard love," for the trainer has one goal in mind—to create the space for the participant to help himself, by finding his own truths. The Trainer/Participant association is a modern-day version of the Zen Master/Student association. The Seminar Training is (as is Zen) a process of seeking to find in self, opposed to ceremony or doctrine, the path to wisdom.

Zen is neither a religion nor a philosophy, but a way of liberation. It is a game of discovering who you are beneath your fear programming. The Zen Master often used a stick to hit a student who wasn't "getting it." In the Seminars, Sutphen purposely uses attitudes and words as his stick. One participant might react best to shock, another to gentle support, another to regression awareness, et cetera. The trainer must do this even at the cost of incurring the participant's dislike.

As in Zen, the participant is encouraged to leap into the unknown and find the True Self within. The True Self is found when the false self is renounced. To accomplish the goal, the trainer must jolt participants out of their intellectual ruts, passe notions, views and convictions that are restricting their lives.

Most of the dialogues in this book are from **The Bushido Training®** and a few are from **The Master of Life Training®**, an updated and gentler version of **Bushido®** which Dick began conducting in 1986. The seminars are usually conducted in approximately 24 cities every year. Dick also offers an annual professional seminar to teach people to become hypnotists and trainers. A week-long **Master of Life Transcendence Training** is held every July and features top-name guests in the human potential and New Age fields.

Write for a free copy of *Master of Life®* magazine. It is published quarterly and contains many articles, plus complete listings of Dick Sutphen's books, tapes and seminars. The magazine is sent free for a year to everyone attending a seminar or purchasing Valley of the Sun tapes: hypnosis, meditation, sleep programming, subliminal programming, symbol therapy, Seminars on Tape, children's programming and a complete line of New Age music.

Sutphen Corporation
Valley of the Sun Publishing
Box 38, Malibu, CA 90265

If you've been served by reading Dick Sutphen's **Master of Life Manual,** you'll be interested in moving on to his **Enlightenment Transcripts.** It takes up where **Master of Life Manual** leaves off. The 36 fast-reading dialogues simplify complicated concepts so they become more easily understood.

In **Enlightenment Transcripts,** Dick explores more on the subject of "aliveness" and combines science and metaphysics to show why you should incorporate challenge into your life. Unconditional love is made workable and logical, and karma is explored in much greater depth. Also: The four questions to ask yourself to let go of fear-based emotions. Sex and spirituality. The three kinds of guilt and how to resolve them. The ultimate thought-stopping technique to end guilt and fear thoughts. And an extension of the Universal Law of Resistance is explored— "That which you resist, you become." There is much, much more in the dialogues, and a complete section titled "How To End Suffering And Attain Peace of Mind." Paperback, 128 pages. . . . . $3.95.

Dick Sutphen's books are available in most metaphysical/New Age stores, or you may obtain them directly from Valley of the Sun Publishing, Box 38, Malibu, CA 90265. Add $1.50 per order for shipping and handling.

Additional Titles of Interest by Dick Sutphen

Past-Life Therapy in Action (1983)—$2.95
Sedona: Psychic Energy Vortexes (1986)—$7.95
**Assertiveness Training and How To
Instantly Read People** (1978, 1983)—$2.95

About The Author

Dick Sutphen (pronounced **Sut-fen**) is an author, hypnotist and seminar trainer. He has authored 37 books for the self-help, human potential and professional advertising markets for publishers such as Simon & Schuster Pocket Books, McGraw-Hill, Crown Publishing, W. H. Allen (England) and his own publishing company, Valley of the Sun His bestselling books, **You Were Born Again To Be Together, Past Lives, Future Loves** and **Unseen Influences** have become classic metaphysical/ self-help titles (Simon & Schuster Pocket Books).

As an author and the developer of innovative group hypnosis exploration techniques that are now being used internationally, Sutphen has appeared on many TV shows such as **The Phil Donahue Show, Good Morning America** and **Tom Snyder's NBC Tomorrow Show.** A two-hour **David Susskind Show** was built around Dick's work and is still being rerun years later as one of the series' most popular programs. He has appeared on over 400 local or regional radio and television shows all over the country.

Sutphen has a 20-year-background in human-potential exploration and hypnosis that includes being the founder and former director of a hypnosis center in Scottsdale, Arizona. Today, he conducts his world-famous seminar trainings throughout the country. Since 1977, more than 60,000 people have attended a Sutphen Seminar, including scores of medical professionals who attend his intensive, week-long **Professional Hypnotist Training** seminars each year. Sutphen's seminar schedule also consists of one- and two-day trainings in approximately 24 cities each year.